C++ Programming Essentials: Theory Concepts And Practical Applications

Anshuman Mishra

Published by Anshuman Mishra, 2025.

C++ PROGRAMMING ESSENTIALS: THEORY, CONCEPTS, AND PRACTICAL APPLICATIONS IS A COMPREHENSIVE GUIDE FOR LEARNING C++ PROGRAMMING, DESIGNED FOR BOTH BEGINNERS AND INTERMEDIATE PROGRAMMERS. THE BOOK COVERS FOUNDATIONAL PRINCIPLES, THEORETICAL CONCEPTS, AND PRACTICAL APPLICATIONS OF C++ PROGRAMMING, MAKING IT AN EXCELLENT RESOURCE FOR STUDENTS, PROFESSIONALS, AND ANYONE SEEKING TO MASTER C++.

THE BOOK IS STRUCTURED TO GRADUALLY INTRODUCE KEY PROGRAMMING CONCEPTS, STARTING WITH THE BASICS AND PROGRESSING TOWARD MORE ADVANCED TOPICS SUCH AS OBJECT-ORIENTED PROGRAMMING (OOP), MEMORY MANAGEMENT, FILE HANDLING, AND EXCEPTION HANDLING. IT ALSO EXPLORES ESSENTIAL CONCEPTS LIKE DATA TYPES, VARIABLES, ARRAYS, FUNCTIONS, POINTERS, CLASSES, INHERITANCE, AND POLYMORPHISM, ENSURING A HOLISTIC UNDERSTANDING OF C++.

KEY FEATURES:

1. **CLEAR EXPLANATIONS**: THE BOOK BREAKS DOWN COMPLEX TOPICS INTO DIGESTIBLE PIECES, MAKING THEM EASIER TO UNDERSTAND.
2. **HANDS-ON APPROACH**: EVERY CONCEPT IS PAIRED WITH PRACTICAL EXAMPLES, ENCOURAGING READERS TO EXPERIMENT AND APPLY THEIR KNOWLEDGE THROUGH CODING EXERCISES.
3. **COMPREHENSIVE COVERAGE**: FROM THE HISTORY OF C AND C++ TO ADVANCED OOP TOPICS LIKE INHERITANCE, POLYMORPHISM, AND EXCEPTION HANDLING, THIS BOOK COVERS EVERYTHING YOU NEED TO KNOW TO EXCEL IN C++ PROGRAMMING.
4. **IN-DEPTH TOPICS**: IT ADDRESSES BOTH THE THEORY AND PRACTICAL ASPECTS OF C++ TO BUILD BOTH A STRONG CONCEPTUAL FOUNDATION AND REAL-WORLD CODING SKILLS.
5. **STEP-BY-STEP APPROACH**: EACH CHAPTER INTRODUCES CONCEPTS SYSTEMATICALLY, WITH EXAMPLES, DETAILED EXPLANATIONS, AND PROBLEMS TO SOLVE, ENSURING STEADY PROGRESS AND RETENTION OF KNOWLEDGE.

BENEFITS OF STUDYING THIS BOOK:

1. **COMPREHENSIVE LEARNING PATH**: THIS BOOK PROVIDES A STRUCTURED APPROACH TO LEARNING C++. STARTING FROM THE BASICS, YOU'LL UNDERSTAND THE HISTORY OF C AND C++, THE SYNTAX, AND HOW C++

EVOLVED INTO A POWERFUL OBJECT-ORIENTED PROGRAMMING LANGUAGE. IT COVERS ESSENTIAL TOPICS LIKE VARIABLES, OPERATORS, FUNCTIONS, ARRAYS, AND DATA TYPES IN THE BEGINNING, ENSURING THAT YOU BUILD A STRONG FOUNDATION BEFORE MOVING INTO MORE COMPLEX AREAS LIKE MEMORY ALLOCATION, POINTERS, INHERITANCE, AND POLYMORPHISM.

2. **HANDS-ON EXPERIENCE**: WITH PRACTICAL EXAMPLES IN EVERY CHAPTER, THIS BOOK HELPS YOU TRANSFORM THEORETICAL KNOWLEDGE INTO REAL-WORLD PROGRAMMING SKILLS. YOU'LL GET AN OPPORTUNITY TO WRITE AND RUN CODE, WHICH IS CRUCIAL TO MASTERING C++ AND PROGRAMMING IN GENERAL.

3. **MASTER OBJECT-ORIENTED PROGRAMMING (OOP)**: ONE OF THE KEY STRENGTHS OF C++ IS ITS ABILITY TO SUPPORT OBJECT-ORIENTED PROGRAMMING. THIS BOOK PROVIDES DETAILED COVERAGE OF OOP CONCEPTS, INCLUDING CLASSES, INHERITANCE, POLYMORPHISM, AND EXCEPTION HANDLING. THESE TOPICS ARE VITAL FOR BUILDING EFFICIENT AND SCALABLE APPLICATIONS.

4. **IN-DEPTH COVERAGE OF POINTERS & MEMORY MANAGEMENT**: UNDERSTANDING POINTERS AND MEMORY MANAGEMENT IS CRUCIAL FOR EFFICIENT PROGRAMMING IN C++. THIS BOOK EXPLAINS THESE TOPICS THOROUGHLY, HELPING YOU AVOID COMMON PITFALLS AND DEVELOP PROGRAMS THAT ARE BOTH POWERFUL AND MEMORY-EFFICIENT.

5. **PREPARING FOR REAL-WORLD APPLICATION DEVELOPMENT**: BY THE END OF THE BOOK, YOU'LL HAVE THE NECESSARY SKILLS TO WRITE COMPLEX, EFFICIENT, AND MAINTAINABLE C++ CODE. THE KNOWLEDGE GAINED FROM STUDYING THIS BOOK WILL BE DIRECTLY APPLICABLE TO REAL-WORLD SOFTWARE DEVELOPMENT, MAKING IT IDEAL FOR THOSE PURSUING CAREERS IN SOFTWARE ENGINEERING, GAME DEVELOPMENT, OR SYSTEMS PROGRAMMING.

C++ PROGRAMMING ESSENTIALS THEORY, CONCEPTS AND PRACTICAL APPLICATIONS

ABOUT THE AUTHOR

ANSHUMAN KUMAR MISHRA IS AN ASSISTANT PROFESSOR AT DORANDA COLLEGE, RANCHI. HE HOLDS AN MTECH IN COMPUTER SCIENCE AND HAS AN EXTENSIVE 18 YEARS OF TEACHING EXPERIENCE IN THE FIELD. HIS EXPERTISE LIES IN COMPUTER PROGRAMMING, ESPECIALLY IN LANGUAGES SUCH AS C++ AND JAVA, AND HE IS DEDICATED TO FOSTERING A DEEP UNDERSTANDING OF PROGRAMMING CONCEPTS AMONG HIS STUDENTS. WITH A PASSION FOR TEACHING AND A COMMITMENT TO EDUCATIONAL EXCELLENCE, ANSHUMAN KUMAR MISHRA HAS CONTRIBUTED SIGNIFICANTLY TO THE DEVELOPMENT OF BOTH UNDERGRADUATE AND POSTGRADUATE STUDENTS. THIS BOOK IS A CULMINATION OF HIS VAST EXPERIENCE IN TEACHING C++ PROGRAMMING AND HIS DEDICATION TO MAKING COMPLEX TOPICS ACCESSIBLE TO STUDENTS.

DR. KUMARI SADHANA MISHRA IS ALSO AN ASSISTANT PROFESSOR AT DORANDA COLLEGE, RANCHI. SHE HAS COMPLETED HER MTECH IN COMPUTER SCIENCE AND BRINGS 15 YEARS OF VALUABLE TEACHING EXPERIENCE. HER PROFOUND UNDERSTANDING OF COMPUTER SCIENCE CONCEPTS AND HER ABILITY TO EXPLAIN COMPLEX TOPICS IN A SIMPLE, STUDENT-FRIENDLY MANNER MAKE HER AN ASSET IN THE ACADEMIC FIELD. AS THE CO-AUTHOR OF THIS BOOK, DR. SADHANA MISHRA HAS CONTRIBUTED SIGNIFICANTLY TO THE DEVELOPMENT OF THE CONTENT, ENSURING THAT STUDENTS GAIN BOTH THEORETICAL KNOWLEDGE AND PRACTICAL SKILLS IN C++ PROGRAMMING.

TOGETHER, ANSHUMAN KUMAR MISHRA AND DR. KUMARI SADHANA MISHRA HAVE CRAFTED THIS BOOK TO SERVE AS A COMPREHENSIVE GUIDE FOR BCA, MCA, BTECH, AND COMPETITIVE STUDENTS, AS WELL AS CBCS STUDENTS, HELPING THEM MASTER THE ESSENTIAL CONCEPTS AND APPLICATIONS OF C++ PROGRAMMING.

"C++ Programming code should be written for developers to comprehend, and only incidentally for the compiler to execute."

— **Anshuman Mishra**

HOW TO STUDY THIS BOOK:

1. **FOLLOW THE STRUCTURE**: THE BOOK IS DESIGNED WITH A PROGRESSIVE STRUCTURE, WHERE EACH CHAPTER BUILDS ON PREVIOUS ONES. BEGIN FROM CHAPTER 1 AND MOVE FORWARD, ENSURING THAT YOU THOROUGHLY UNDERSTAND EACH CONCEPT BEFORE MOVING TO THE NEXT. SKIPPING CHAPTERS OR SECTIONS MIGHT RESULT IN MISSING OUT ON CRUCIAL FOUNDATIONAL KNOWLEDGE.

2. **HANDS-ON PRACTICE**: AS YOU READ THROUGH THE CHAPTERS, IT IS CRUCIAL TO WRITE THE CODE EXAMPLES ON YOUR OWN. USE AN INTEGRATED DEVELOPMENT ENVIRONMENT (IDE) LIKE VISUAL STUDIO, CODE::BLOCKS, OR XCODE TO COMPILE AND EXECUTE THE PROGRAMS. EXPERIMENT WITH THE EXAMPLES TO BETTER UNDERSTAND HOW EACH CONCEPT WORKS.

3. **REVIEW AND SOLVE EXERCISES**: AT THE END OF EACH CHAPTER, THERE ARE EXERCISES THAT TEST YOUR UNDERSTANDING. COMPLETE THESE EXERCISES TO REINFORCE THE CONCEPTS AND IMPROVE YOUR PROBLEM-SOLVING SKILLS. TRY TO CHALLENGE YOURSELF BY SOLVING PROBLEMS THAT WERE NOT DIRECTLY COVERED IN THE BOOK.

4. **TAKE NOTES**: WHILE READING, TAKE NOTES TO SUMMARIZE KEY CONCEPTS, ESPECIALLY WHEN WORKING THROUGH COMPLEX IDEAS LIKE POINTERS, MEMORY ALLOCATION, AND OBJECT-ORIENTED PROGRAMMING. WRITING NOTES CAN HELP REINFORCE LEARNING AND ACT AS A QUICK REFERENCE GUIDE WHEN YOU ARE CODING.

5. **LEARN BY DEBUGGING**: DEBUGGING IS A VITAL SKILL FOR ANY PROGRAMMER. WHILE STUDYING THIS BOOK, IF YOU ENCOUNTER ERRORS OR UNEXPECTED RESULTS, TAKE TIME TO DEBUG THE CODE AND UNDERSTAND WHAT WENT WRONG. DEBUGGING WILL HELP YOU GRASP THE INNER WORKINGS OF C++ MORE EFFECTIVELY.

6. **USE ADDITIONAL RESOURCES**: FOR MORE COMPLEX TOPICS, SUCH AS ADVANCED MEMORY MANAGEMENT OR FUNCTION OVERLOADING, IT CAN BE BENEFICIAL TO SUPPLEMENT THE BOOK WITH OTHER LEARNING RESOURCES, LIKE ONLINE TUTORIALS, FORUMS, AND C++ DOCUMENTATION.

7. **APPLY WHAT YOU LEARN**: ONCE YOU'VE MASTERED THE CONCEPTS IN THE BOOK, APPLY THEM BY WORKING ON PERSONAL PROJECTS. TRY DEVELOPING SMALL APPLICATIONS, ALGORITHMS, OR GAMES USING THE C++ CONCEPTS YOU'VE LEARNED. THIS WILL HELP SOLIDIFY YOUR KNOWLEDGE AND PREPARE YOU FOR REAL-WORLD DEVELOPMENT TASKS.

IN CONCLUSION, *"C++ PROGRAMMING ESSENTIALS"* IS A MUST-HAVE RESOURCE FOR ANYONE LOOKING TO DIVE DEEP INTO C++ PROGRAMMING. WITH ITS CLEAR EXPLANATIONS, PRACTICAL EXAMPLES, AND COMPREHENSIVE COVERAGE OF ESSENTIAL TOPICS, IT PROVIDES THE TOOLS NECESSARY TO SUCCEED IN C++ PROGRAMMING. BY FOLLOWING THE STRUCTURED LEARNING PATH, PRACTICING CONSISTENTLY, AND SOLVING CHALLENGES, YOU'LL DEVELOP THE SKILLS REQUIRED TO BECOME PROFICIENT IN C++ AND APPLY IT IN REAL-WORLD APPLICATIONS

Copyright Page

Title C++ PROGRAMMING ESSENTIALS THEORY, CONCEPTS AND PRACTICAL APPLICATIONS

TOPICS

CHAPTER-1

INTRODUCTION TO C AND C++

1. History of C and C++
Definition

1. **C Language:**
   o **Developed By:** Dennis Ritchie at Bell Laboratories in 1972.
   o **Purpose:** Initially designed to create the UNIX operating system, making it portable and efficient.
   o **Nature:**
      ▪ A **procedural programming language**, meaning it follows a structured step-by-step approach.
      ▪ Known for being a middle-level language: it bridges the gap between high-level languages (like Python) and low-level assembly languages.
   o **Impact:**
      ▪ Became the foundation for many programming languages, including C++, Java, and Python.
      ▪ Still widely used in system programming, embedded systems, and applications requiring performance and direct hardware interaction.

2. **C++ Language:**
   o **Developed By:** Bjarne Stroustrup in 1983 at Bell Labs.
   o **Purpose:** Introduced to extend the capabilities of C by adding **object-oriented programming (OOP)** features.
   o **Nature:**
      ▪ A **multi-paradigm language**, combining procedural and object-oriented paradigms.
      ▪ Adds features like **classes, objects, inheritance, polymorphism, and encapsulation**.
   o **Impact:**
      ▪ Widely used in software development for complex applications like game engines, GUI-based applications, and real-time systems.

Concept

1. **C Language Concepts:**
   o **Procedural Programming:**
      ▪ Programs are a sequence of functions and procedures that operate on data.
      ▪ Focuses on dividing the program into smaller parts (functions), which are executed sequentially.
   o **Data and Code Separation:**
      ▪ Data is kept separate from functions, making the logic clear but less modular.

o **Use Cases:** System programming, embedded systems, and programs requiring high performance.

2. **C++ Language Concepts:**
   o **Object-Oriented Programming (OOP):**
     - Focuses on creating objects that combine data and the functions that operate on the data into a single unit.
     - Key features include:
       - **Encapsulation:** Combining data and methods in a class.
       - **Inheritance:** Reusing and extending existing classes.
       - **Polymorphism:** Using a single interface to represent different data types or classes.
   o **Multi-Paradigm:**
     - Supports procedural, object-oriented, and generic programming (templates).
   o **Use Cases:** Games, simulations, database systems, GUI applications, and large-scale software.

Key Differences Between C and C++

Aspect	C	C++
Programming Paradigm	Procedural Programming	Object-Oriented + Procedural
Focus	Functions and Procedures	Objects and Classes
Inheritance	Not Supported	Supported
Encapsulation	Not Supported	Supported
Data Handling	Data and functions are separate.	Data and functions are combined in objects.
Abstraction	Not directly supported.	Supported via classes and objects.
Security	Less secure (global data is accessible).	More secure (data can be private).
Extensibility	Difficult to extend functionality.	Easy to extend functionality using inheritance.

Aspect	C	C++
Use Cases	System programming, embedded systems.	Application development, games, GUIs.

Detailed Explanation of Key Features

1. **Procedural Programming (C):**
   - Program execution flows sequentially from top to bottom.
   - Functions are used to implement logic, and each function performs a specific task.
   - Example:

```c
#include <stdio.h>

int addNumbers(int a, int b) {
    return a + b;
}

int main() {
    int result = addNumbers(5, 10);
    printf("Result: %d\n", result);
    return 0;
}
```

   Output:

```
Result: 15
```

2. **Object-Oriented Programming (C++):**
   - Combines data and methods into **classes** and **objects**.
   - Example:

```cpp
#include <iostream>
using namespace std;

class Calculator {
    public:
        int add(int a, int b) {
            return a + b;
        }
};

int main() {
    Calculator calc;
    cout << "Result: " << calc.add(5, 10) << endl;
    return 0;
}
```

Output:

```
Result: 15
```

Procedural Programming (PP):

- Focuses on functions or procedures to perform tasks.
- Example Languages: C, Pascal.
- **Characteristics:**
  - Sequential flow.
  - Use of variables, loops, and conditionals.
  - Example: Function to calculate factorial in C.

Object-Oriented Programming (OOP):

- Focuses on objects and their interactions.
- Example Languages: C++, Java.
- **Characteristics:**
  - Encapsulation, Inheritance, Polymorphism, and Abstraction.
  - Code reuse and modularity.
  - Example: Class to represent a Student.

---

3. Using main() Function

Definition:

- The `main()` function is the entry point of any C or C++ program.
- Syntax:

```
int main() {
    // Code
    return 0;
}
```

Concept:

- **Purpose of `main`:** The operating system calls `main()` to start the program execution.
- `return 0;`: Indicates successful program termination.

Steps to Compile and Execute:

1. Write code in a text editor (e.g., Notepad++, VS Code).
2. Save with `.cpp` extension.
3. Compile using a compiler like GCC or G++:

   ```
   g++ program.cpp -o program
   ```

4. Run the compiled program:

Practical Examples with Solutions and Output

Example 1: A Simple C++ Program

Code:

```cpp
#include <iostream>
using namespace std;

int main() {
    cout << "Hello, World!" << endl;
    return 0;}
```

Output:

```
Hello, World!
```

Explanation:

- `#include <iostream>`: Includes standard input/output library.
- `cout`: Outputs text to the console.
- `return 0`: Signals successful execution.

Example 2: Procedural Programming - Sum of Two Numbers

Code:

```
#include <stdio.h>

int main() {
    int a, b, sum;
    printf("Enter two numbers: ");
    scanf("%d %d", &a, &b);
    sum = a + b;
    printf("Sum = %d\n", sum);
    return 0;}
```

Output:

```
Enter two numbers: 5 10
Sum = 15
```

Explanation:

Procedural approach: The task is completed step by step using functions like `scanf` and `printf`.

Example 3: Object-Oriented Programming - Class Example

Code:

```
#include <iostream>
using namespace std;

class Rectangle {
    public:
        int length, width;

        int calculateArea() {
            return length * width;
        }
};

int main() {
    Rectangle rect;
    rect.length = 10;
    rect.width = 5;

    cout << "Area of Rectangle: " << rect.calculateArea() << endl;
    return 0;}
```

Output:

```
Area of Rectangle: 50
```

Explanation:

- Encapsulation: Data (`length`, `width`) and methods (`calculateArea`) are encapsulated within the `Rectangle` class.

Example 4: Using Loops in Procedural Programming

Code:

```
#include <stdio.h>

int main() {
    for (int i = 1; i <= 5; i++) {
        printf("Number: %d\n", i);      }
    return 0;}
```

Output:

```
Number: 1
Number: 2
Number: 3
Number: 4
Number: 5
```

Explanation:

- Loops are a key feature of procedural programming to execute repetitive tasks.

Example 5: Object-Oriented Approach with Constructor

Code:

```
#include <iostream>
using namespace std;

class Circle {
    public:
        double radius;

        // Constructor
        Circle(double r) {
            radius = r;
        }
```

```
        double calculateArea() {
            return 3.14 * radius * radius;
        }
};

int main() {
    Circle circle(5.0); // Creating an object
    cout << "Area of Circle: " << circle.calculateArea() << endl;
    return 0;
}
```

Output:

```
Area of Circle: 78.5
```

Explanation:

- Constructor initializes `radius` when the object `circle` is created.
- The object-oriented paradigm promotes reusability and modularity.

Additional Key Takeaways

- **C is simple and efficient:**
  - Known for its simplicity and close-to-hardware nature, making it ideal for **system programming**, **operating systems**, **embedded systems**, and **real-time applications**.
  - Offers **fine control over memory** using pointers and dynamic memory allocation, which is vital for performance-critical applications.
- **C++ extends functionality with abstraction:**
  - Provides **modularity** through classes and objects, making code easier to maintain and debug.
  - Introduces **abstraction**, allowing complex systems to be represented in a simplified and understandable way.
- **Reusability and scalability in C++:**
  - Features like **inheritance** and **polymorphism** promote reusability, enabling developers to build large, scalable applications.
  - Facilitates the creation of **libraries** and reusable modules for widespread use in software development.
- **Programming Paradigm Shifts:**
  - **Procedural Programming (C):** Best for small, linear problems with well-defined steps.
  - **Object-Oriented Programming (C++):** Ideal for complex, dynamic problems where modular design and reusability are essential.

- **Wide Application Range:**
  - **C:** Used in areas like operating system kernels, device drivers, and microcontroller programming.
  - **C++:** Common in game development, simulation software, GUI-based applications, and financial systems.
- **Backward Compatibility:**
  - C++ maintains compatibility with C, allowing developers to use C libraries and functions within C++ programs. This provides flexibility in leveraging legacy systems.
- **Learning Path for Programmers:**
  - Starting with **C** builds a strong foundation in programming logic and memory management.
  - Transitioning to **C++** introduces higher-level programming concepts like object-oriented design, preparing developers for advanced technologies.
- **Problem-Solving Focus:**
  - **C:** Encourages thinking in terms of algorithms and efficient resource utilization.
  - **C++:** Promotes structured problem-solving by dividing problems into manageable components through **classes** and **objects**.
- **Community and Ecosystem:**
  - Both languages have vast communities, robust support, and numerous libraries for developers to use and learn from.
- **Understanding Real-World Examples:**
  - Examples like file handling, database management, and user-defined data structures demonstrate how procedural (C) and object-oriented (C++) approaches differ in tackling real-world problems.

- **Versatility of C++:**
  - Supports **generic programming** using templates, enabling code to work with any data type.
  - Offers **exception handling**, making it easier to write robust and error-resilient programs.
- **Critical Thinking Development:**
  - Learning the strengths and weaknesses of both languages helps develop a **problem-oriented mindset**, enabling you to choose the right tools for specific tasks.
- **Modern Relevance:**
  - C++ continues to evolve with features from modern programming trends (e.g., **C++11**, **C++17**, and **C++20**), ensuring it remains relevant for high-performance and enterprise-grade software.

By grasping these points, developers can better understand where and how to apply C and C++ effectively, strengthening their programming and problem-solving skills.

25 MCQ ON THESE TOPICS

1. History of C and C++

1. Who is considered the father of the C programming language?
   a) Dennis Ritchie
   b) Bjarne Stroustrup
   c) James Gosling
   d) Guido van Rossum
   Answer: a
2. C programming language was developed in the year:
   a) 1970
   b) 1972
   c) 1983
   d) 1991
   Answer: b
3. Who developed C++?
   a) Dennis Ritchie
   b) Bjarne Stroustrup
   c) Anders Hejlsberg
   d) Ken Thompson
   Answer: b
4. The original name of C++ was:
   a) C with Classes
   b) New C
   c) Object-Oriented C
   d) Enhanced C
   Answer: a
5. What year was C++ standardized by ISO?
   a) 1985
   b) 1990
   c) 1998
   d) 2000
   Answer: c

2. Overview of Procedural Programming and Object-Oriented Programming

6. Procedural programming focuses on:
   a) Objects
   b) Functions and procedures
   c) Classes
   d) Inheritance
   Answer: b

7. Which of the following is not a feature of Object-Oriented Programming?
   a) Encapsulation
   b) Polymorphism
   c) Recursion
   d) Inheritance
   Answer: c
8. What is the primary difference between procedural and object-oriented programming?
   a) Use of functions vs. objects
   b) Use of global variables
   c) Execution speed
   d) Compiler differences
   Answer: a
9. Encapsulation in OOP refers to:
   a) Breaking a program into functions
   b) Hiding data and methods
   c) Using inheritance
   d) Creating multiple objects
   Answer: b
10. Which feature of OOP allows a derived class to use the properties of a base class?
    a) Abstraction
    b) Encapsulation
    c) Inheritance
    d) Polymorphism
    Answer: c

3. Using main() Function

11. The correct syntax of the main() function in C++ is:
    a) int main();
    b) void main();
    c) main();
    d) None of the above
    Answer: a
12. What is the return type of main() in C++?
    a) void
    b) int
    c) float
    d) double
    Answer: b

13. In C++, what value is usually returned by the main() function upon successful execution?
    a) 1
    b) -1
    c) 0
    d) None
    Answer: c
14. Which header file is typically included in a C++ program?
    a) #include <main.h>
    b) #include <iostream>
    c) #include <stdio.h>
    d) #include <program.h>
    Answer: b
15. Which statement correctly ends the execution of the main() function?
    a) exit();
    b) return;
    c) return 0;
    d) None of the above
    Answer: c

4. Compiling and Executing Simple Programs in C++

16. Which command is used to compile a C++ program?
    a) g++
    b) gcc
    c) cppc
    d) run++
    Answer: a
17. What file extension is used for a C++ source file?
    a) .c
    b) .cpp
    c) .cp
    d) .h
    Answer: b
18. What is the purpose of the `#include` directive in C++?
    a) To include header files
    b) To define variables
    c) To declare functions
    d) To include main()
    Answer: a
19. Which of the following is the correct way to print output in C++?
    a) printf();
    b) print();
    c) cout << "";

d) System.out.println();
Answer: c

20. If a C++ program contains errors, the compiler:
    a) Ignores the errors and runs the program
    b) Displays error messages
    c) Automatically fixes the errors
    d) None of the above
    Answer: b

Additional Questions

21. What does the << operator do in C++?
    a) Adds two numbers
    b) Outputs data to the console
    c) Reads input from the console
    d) None of the above
    Answer: b

22. What is the role of the `main()` function in a C++ program?
    a) To initialize variables
    b) To define classes
    c) To serve as the entry point of the program
    d) To include libraries
    Answer: c

23. What does `g++ -o program program.cpp` do?
    a) Runs the program
    b) Compiles the program to an executable named `program`
    c) Deletes the program file
    d) Creates a new source file
    Answer: b

24. Which of the following is not a valid C++ keyword?
    a) private
    b) public
    c) protected
    d) function
    Answer: d

25. Which character is used to terminate a statement in C++?
    a) .
    b) ,
    c) ;
    d) :
    Answer: c

CHAPTER-2

DATA TYPES, VARIABLES, CONSTANTS, OPERATORS, AND BASIC I/O

1 Declaring a Variable

- A declaration tells the compiler about the **type** of the variable and its **name**.
- At this point, no memory is allocated for the variable's value, only its type and scope are specified.

Example:

```
int age; // Declares a variable named 'age' of type integer.
float pi; // Declares a variable named 'pi' of type float.
char grade; // Declares a variable named 'grade' of type character.
```

Defining a Variable

- When a variable is **defined**, memory is allocated for storing its value.
- In many programming languages like C and C++, declaring and defining are often done together, but they are conceptually different.
- In separate declaration and definition:
  - o **Declaration:** Acts as a reference to the variable.
  - o **Definition:** Allocates memory and assigns an initial value if required.

Example:

```
extern int age; // Declaration (no memory allocated yet).
int age = 30;   // Definition (memory allocated and value assigned).
```

Initializing a Variable

- **Initialization** assigns an initial value to the variable at the time of its definition.
- Variables must be initialized before use, or they may hold garbage values.
- Initialization can be done directly at the point of declaration:

Example:

```
int age = 25;    // Integer variable initialized with 25.
float pi = 3.14; // Floating-point variable initialized with 3.14.
char grade = 'A'; // Character variable initialized with 'A'.
```

- Variables that are declared but not initialized can hold **undefined garbage values**.
- Always initialize variables to avoid logical errors.

Example:

1. Uninitialized Variable

```
#include <iostream>
using namespace std;

int main() {
    int num; // Uninitialized variable
    cout << "Value of num: " << num << endl; // Undefined (garbage value)
    return 0;
}
```

2. Declaring and Initializing Integer Variables

```
#include <iostream>
using namespace std;

int main() {
    int age;           // Declaration
    age = 25;          // Definition and initialization
    cout << "Age: " << age << endl; // Output: Age: 25
    return 0;
}
```

3. Combining Declaration and Initialization

```
#include <iostream>
using namespace std;

int main() {
    int marks = 95; // Declaration and initialization together
    cout << "Marks: " << marks << endl; // Output: Marks: 95
    return 0;
}
```

4. Global Variable Declaration and Definition

```
#include <iostream>
using namespace std;

extern int count; // Declaration (visible to all files)

int count = 10;    // Definition (memory allocated here)

int main() {
    cout << "Count: " << count << endl; // Output: Count: 10
```

```
    return 0;
}
```

5. Initializing Multiple Variables

```
#include <iostream>
using namespace std;

int main() {
    int a = 10, b = 20, c = 30; // Multiple variables initialized in one
line
    cout << "a: " << a << ", b: " << b << ", c: " << c << endl; // Output:
a: 10, b: 20, c: 30
    return 0;
}
```

6. Float and Character Initialization

```
#include <iostream>
using namespace std;

int main() {
    float pi = 3.14159;
    char grade = 'A';
    cout << "Value of pi: " << pi << endl; // Output: Value of pi: 3.14159
    cout << "Grade: " << grade << endl;    // Output: Grade: A
    return 0;
}
```

By **declaring**, **defining**, and **initializing variables** effectively, we ensure memory allocation and proper data handling in programs.

2. Scope of Variables and Named Constants

- **Scope:** Defines where a variable can be accessed.
    - o **Global Scope:** Variables declared outside functions and accessible throughout the program.
    - o **Local Scope:** Variables declared within a function or block and only accessible within it.
    - o **Block Scope:** Variables declared within { } and accessible only inside those braces.
- **Named Constants:** Declared using const or #define to make values immutable.
    - o Example in C++:

        ```
        const float PI = 3.14;
        #define MAX 100
        ```

3. Keywords and Data Types

Keywords

- Keywords are **reserved words** in a programming language that have a predefined meaning.
- They **cannot** be used as variable names, function names, or identifiers.
- Keywords define the **syntax and structure** of the program.

Examples of C Keywords:

- `int`, `float`, `char`, `void`, `if`, `else`, `while`, `for`, `return`, `switch`, `break`, `continue`, `sizeof`, etc.

Examples of C++ Keywords (includes all C keywords + new ones):

- `class`, `this`, `namespace`, `virtual`, `try`, `catch`, `throw`, `private`, `public`, `protected`, `friend`, etc.

Practical Example of Keywords Usage

1. **Using `if`, `else`, and `return` Keywords in C:**

```
#include <stdio.h>
int main() {
    int number = 5;
    if (number % 2 == 0) {   // 'if' keyword
        printf("Even number\n");
    } else {                 // 'else' keyword
        printf("Odd number\n");
    }
    return 0;               // 'return' keyword
}
```

Output:

```
Odd number
```

2. **Using Keywords in C++ (class, public, private):**

```
#include <iostream>
using namespace std;

class Car {          // 'class' keyword
private:
    string brand;    // 'private' keyword
public:
    void setBrand(string b) { brand = b; } // 'public' keyword
    void getBrand() { cout << "Car Brand: " << brand << endl; }
};
```

```
int main() {
    Car car;
    car.setBrand("Toyota");
    car.getBrand();
    return 0;
}
```

Output:

```
Car Brand: Toyota
```

Data Types

- **Definition:** Data types specify the type of data that a variable can hold, defining the **size**, **range**, and **operations** permissible on it.
- C and C++ offer a variety of data types categorized as **primary**, **derived**, and **user-defined**.

1. Primary Data Types

These are the **basic built-in data types**:

- `int` - Integer (whole numbers, both positive and negative).
- `float` - Single-precision floating-point numbers.
- `double` - Double-precision floating-point numbers.
- `char` - Character data type (stores single characters).
- `void` - Represents absence of value (used in functions that return nothing).

Examples:

1. Basic Data Types Example

```
#include <iostream>
using namespace std;

int main() {
    int age = 25;           // Integer variable
    float height = 5.8;     // Float variable
    char grade = 'A';       // Character variable
    double pi = 3.1415926535; // Double variable

    cout << "Age: " << age << endl;
    cout << "Height: " << height << endl;
    cout << "Grade: " << grade << endl;
    cout << "Value of Pi: " << pi << endl;
```

```
        return 0;
    }
```

Output:

```
Age: 25
Height: 5.8
Grade: A
Value of Pi: 3.1415926535
```

2. Derived Data Types

- **Array Example in C++**

```
#include <iostream>
using namespace std;

int main() {
    int arr[5] = {10, 20, 30, 40, 50};

    for (int i = 0; i < 5; i++) {
        cout << "Element " << i << ": " << arr[i] << endl;
    }

    return 0;
}
```

Output:

```
Element 0: 10
Element 1: 20
Element 2: 30
Element 3: 40
Element 4: 50
```

- **Pointer Example in C++**

```
#include <iostream>
using namespace std;

int main() {
    int num = 5;
    int* ptr = &num;

    cout << "Value of num: " << num << endl;
    cout << "Address of num: " << ptr << endl;

    return 0;
}
```

Output:

```
Value of num: 5
Address of num: [Memory address]
```

3. User-Defined Data Types

- **Structure Example in C++**

```cpp
#include <iostream>
using namespace std;

struct Student {
    int id;
    char name[50];
    float marks;
};

int main() {
    Student student1 = {1, "John Doe", 87.5};

    cout << "ID: " << student1.id << ", Name: " << student1.name << ",
Marks: " << student1.marks << endl;

    return 0;
}
```

Output:

```
ID: 1, Name: John Doe, Marks: 87.5
```

4. Casting of Data Types

- **Implicit Casting Example in C++**

```cpp
#include <iostream>
using namespace std;

int main() {
    int a = 5;
    float b = 2.5;
    float result = a + b; // 'a' is implicitly converted to float

    cout << "Result: " << result << endl;

    return 0;
}
```

Output:

```
Result: 7.5
```

2. Explicit Casting (Type Casting)

- **Definition:** Explicit casting is a **manual type conversion** performed by the programmer.
- It uses a **cast operator** to convert one data type into another.
- Explicit casting is necessary when there is potential for data loss or precision reduction, and the programmer takes responsibility for the conversion.

Example in C++:

```
#include <iostream>
using namespace std;

int main() {
    int num = 10;
    float result = (float)num / 3; // Explicitly converting 'num' to float
    cout << "Result: " << result << endl;
    return 0;
}
```

Output:

```
Result: 3.33333
```

Explanation:

- The integer `num` is explicitly cast to `float` using `(float)num`.
- This ensures the division operation results in a floating-point value instead of integer truncation.

Practical Examples of Implicit and Explicit Casting

1. Implicit Casting Example (Type Promotion in Expressions)

```
#include <iostream>
using namespace std;

int main() {
    char c = 'A'; // Character with ASCII value 65
    int asciiValue = c; // Implicitly converts 'char' to 'int'
    cout << "ASCII value of '" << c << "': " << asciiValue << endl;
    return 0;
}
```

Output:

```
ASCII value of 'A': 65
```

2. Explicit Casting Example (Truncation of Float to Integer)

```
#include <iostream>
using namespace std;

int main() {
    float pi = 3.14;
    int truncated = (int)pi; // Explicitly converting float to int
    cout << "Truncated Value: " << truncated << endl;
    return 0;
}
```

Output:

```
Truncated Value: 3
```

Explanation:

- Here, `(int)pi` truncates the fractional part, leaving only the integer portion.

3. Combining Implicit and Explicit Casting:

```
#include <iostream>
using namespace std;

int main() {
    int a = 5, b = 2;
    float result1 = a / b;          // Implicit casting (integer division)
    float result2 = (float)a / b;   // Explicit casting (floating-point
division)

    cout << "Implicit Casting: " << result1 << endl; // Result: 2.0
(truncated)
    cout << "Explicit Casting: " << result2 << endl; // Result: 2.5
    return 0;
}
```

Output:

```
Implicit Casting: 2
Explicit Casting: 2.5
```

5. Operators: Arithmetic, Logical, and Bitwise

1. Arithmetic Operators

- **Definition:** Perform basic mathematical operations such as addition, subtraction, multiplication, division, and modulus.
- **Operators:**
  - + (Addition)
  - – (Subtraction)
  - * (Multiplication)
  - / (Division)
  - % (Modulus - remainder of division)

Example (C):

1. Arithmetic Operators Example (C++)

```
#include <iostream>
using namespace std;

int main() {
    int a = 10, b = 3;
    cout << "Addition: " << a + b << endl;        // 10 + 3 = 13
    cout << "Subtraction: " << a - b << endl;     // 10 - 3 = 7
    cout << "Multiplication: " << a * b << endl;  // 10 * 3 = 30
    cout << "Division: " << a / b << endl;        // 10 / 3 = 3 (integer
division)
    cout << "Modulus: " << a % b << endl;         // 10 % 3 = 1
    return 0;
}
```

Output:

```
Addition: 13
Subtraction: 7
Multiplication: 30
Division: 3
Modulus: 1
```

2. Logical Operators Example (C++)

```
#include <iostream>
using namespace std;

int main() {
    int a = 5, b = 3;
    bool result1 = (a > 3 && b < 5); // true (5 > 3 AND 3 < 5)
    bool result2 = (a < 3 || b < 5); // true (5 < 3 OR 3 < 5)
    bool result3 = !(a == b);        // true (NOT 5 == 3)

    cout << "Logical AND: " << result1 << endl;
```

```
cout << "Logical OR: " << result2 << endl;
cout << "Logical NOT: " << result3 << endl;
return 0;}
```

Output:

```
Logical AND: 1
Logical OR: 1
Logical NOT: 1
```

3. Bitwise Operators

- **Definition:** Perform operations at the binary level, manipulating individual bits of integer values.
- **Operators:**
    - & (Bitwise AND)
    - | (Bitwise OR)
    - ^ (Bitwise XOR)
    - ~ (Bitwise NOT)
    - << (Left Shift)
    - >> (Right Shift)

Example (C++):

```
#include <iostream>
using namespace std;

int main() {
    int a = 5, b = 3; // a = 0101, b = 0011 in binary
    int andResult = a & b;   // Bitwise AND -> 0001 (1)
    int orResult = a | b;    // Bitwise OR -> 0111 (7)
    int xorResult = a ^ b;   // Bitwise XOR -> 0110 (6)
    int notResult = ~a;      // Bitwise NOT -> -(0101 + 1) = -6
    int leftShift = a << 1;  // Left shift -> 1010 (10)
    int rightShift = a >> 1; // Right shift -> 0010 (2)

    cout << "Bitwise AND: " << andResult << endl;
    cout << "Bitwise OR: " << orResult << endl;
    cout << "Bitwise XOR: " << xorResult << endl;
    cout << "Bitwise NOT: " << notResult << endl;
    cout << "Left Shift: " << leftShift << endl;
    cout << "Right Shift: " << rightShift << endl;
    return 0;
}
```

Output:

```
Bitwise AND: 1
Bitwise OR: 7
Bitwise XOR: 6
Bitwise NOT: -6
```

```
Left Shift: 10
Right Shift: 2
```

Detailed Explanation

1. **Bitwise AND (&):**
   - Compares each bit of two operands.
   - Resultant bit is 1 only if both corresponding bits are 1.
   - Example: `5 & 3` → `0101 & 0011 = 0001` → Result = 1.

2. **Bitwise OR (|):**
   - Compares each bit of two operands.
   - Resultant bit is 1 if at least one corresponding bit is 1.
   - Example: `5 | 3` → `0101 | 0011 = 0111` → Result = 7.

3. **Bitwise XOR (^):**
   - Compares each bit of two operands.
   - Resultant bit is 1 if the corresponding bits are different.
   - Example: `5 ^ 3` → `0101 ^ 0011 = 0110` → Result = 6.

4. **Bitwise NOT (~):**
   - Flips each bit of the operand.
   - Example: `~5` → In binary: `0101` → Flipped: `1010` (2's complement form).

5. **Left Shift (<<):**
   - Shifts the bits to the left, filling in zeros on the right.
   - Example: `5 << 1` → `0101` shifted becomes `1010` → Result = 10.

6. **Right Shift (>>):**
   - Shifts the bits to the right, discarding bits on the right.
   - Example: `5 >> 1` → `0101` shifted becomes `0010` → Result = 2.

Key Takeaways

1. **Arithmetic Operators:** Used for numeric calculations.
2. **Logical Operators:** Help in forming conditions and decision-making in programs.
3. **Bitwise Operators:** Work at the binary level for efficient low-level data manipulation.
4. **Use Cases:**
   - Arithmetic for calculations.
   - Logical operators for control flow in programs.
   - Bitwise operators in embedded systems, cryptography, and graphics.

6. Using Comments in Programs

- **Single-line comment:** Begins with `//`.
- **Multi-line comment:** Enclosed in `/* */`.
  - Example:

```
// This is a single-line comment.
/* This is a
   multi-line comment. */
```

7. Character I/O

Character I/O deals with reading and writing single characters using specific functions. In C, character I/O functions include **getc(), putc(), getchar(), and putchar()**.

Functions for Character I/O

1. getc() and putc()

- **Definition:** Used to read and write a single character from/to a file stream.
- **Usage:** Primarily for file operations.
  - `getc()` reads a character from a file stream.
  - `putc()` writes a character to a file stream.

Syntax:

```
int getc(FILE *stream);
int putc(int char, FILE *stream);
```

Example (File I/O):

```
#include <stdio.h>
int main() {
    FILE *file;
    char ch;

    // Open file in write mode
    file = fopen("example.txt", "w");
    if (file == NULL) {
        printf("Error opening file!\n");
        return 1;
    }

    printf("Enter a character to write to the file: ");
    ch = getchar();  // Read character from standard input
    putc(ch, file);  // Write character to the file
    fclose(file);    // Close the file
```

```
    // Open file in read mode
    file = fopen("example.txt", "r");
    if (file == NULL) {
        printf("Error opening file!\n");
        return 1;
    }

    printf("Reading character from the file: ");
    ch = getc(file); // Read character from the file
    putchar(ch);     // Display the character
    fclose(file);

    return 0;  }
```

Output (when input is A):

```
Enter a character to write to the file: A
Reading character from the file: A
```

2. getchar() and putchar()

- **Definition:** Used to read and write characters from/to the standard input/output (keyboard/screen).
    - o   getchar() reads a single character from the standard input.
    - o   putchar() writes a single character to the standard output.

Syntax:

```
int getchar(void);
int putchar(int char);
```

Example (Standard I/O):

```
#include <stdio.h>
int main() {
    char ch;

    printf("Enter a character: ");
    ch = getchar();   // Read a single character from the keyboard
    printf("You entered: ");
    putchar(ch);      // Print the character to the screen

    return 0;
}
```

Output (when input is B):

```
Enter a character: B
You entered: B
```

Explanation of Code

1. **getc()**: Reads a single character from a file. Used for file operations.
2. **putc()**: Writes a single character to a file. Used for file output.
3. **getchar()**: Simplified function for reading a character from standard input (keyboard).
4. **putchar()**: Simplified function for writing a character to standard output (screen).

Key Takeaways

1. **getc() and putc()**: Work with file streams and are often used in file handling.
2. **getchar() and putchar()**: Handle single character input and output for standard streams (keyboard and screen).
3. **Use Cases**:
   - Reading characters from files or user input.
   - Writing characters to files or displaying them on the console.
   - Useful for low-level operations and single-character I/O needs.

8. Formatted and Console I/O

- **In C:**
  - `printf()` for output.
  - `scanf()` for input.
  - Example:

    ```
    int a;
    printf("Enter a number: ");
    scanf("%d", &a);
    printf("You entered: %d", a);
    ```

- **In C++:**
  - `cin` for input and `cout` for output.
  - Example:

    ```
    int a;
    cout << "Enter a number: ";
    cin >> a;
    cout << "You entered: " << a;
    ```

9. Basic Header Files

`stdio.h` (Standard Input/Output)

- **Purpose:** Provides functions for input and output operations, such as reading from and writing to the console or files.
- **Functions:**
    - `printf()`: Used to print formatted output to the console.
    - `scanf()`: Used to read formatted input from the console.
    - `getc()`: Reads a single character from a file stream.
    - `putc()`: Writes a single character to a file stream.
    - `getchar()`: Reads a single character from standard input.
    - `putchar()`: Writes a single character to standard output.
    - `fopen()`: Opens a file for reading or writing.
    - `fclose()`: Closes an opened file.

Example:

```
#include <stdio.h>

int main() {
    int age;
    printf("Enter your age: ");
    scanf("%d", &age);   // User input
    printf("Your age is: %d\n", age);   // Output
    return 0;
}
```

Functions in `stdio.h` are critical for handling text-based input/output in most C programs.

---

2. `iostream.h` (C++ Standard Input/Output)

- **Purpose:** Provides functions for handling input/output using streams in C++.
- **Functions:**
    - `cin`: Standard input stream used to read data.
    - `cout`: Standard output stream used to display data.
    - `cerr`: Standard error stream, used for error messages.
    - `clog`: Standard log stream for logging information.

Important Note: The `iostream.h` header is part of older versions of C++. In modern C++, we use **<iostream>** (without `.h`).

Example:

```
#include <iostream.h>  // Deprecated header, use <iostream> in modern C++

int main() {
    int age;
    cout << "Enter your age: ";
    cin >> age;  // Read input
    cout << "Your age is: " << age << endl;  // Output
    return 0;
}
```

Functions in `iostream.h` are used for stream-based input and output, which is central to C++.

---

3. `conio.h` (Console Input/Output)

- **Purpose:** A non-standard header in C that provides functions to perform console-related operations such as clearing the screen and handling keyboard input without pressing Enter.
- **Functions:**
    - `clrscr()`: Clears the console screen (not available in standard C, often used in Turbo C++ or other compilers).
    - `getch()`: Reads a single character from the keyboard without the need to press Enter.
    - `getche()`: Reads a character and displays it on the screen.
    - `gotoxy(x, y)`: Moves the cursor to the given x, y coordinates on the console.

Example:

```
#include <conio.h>

int main() {
    char ch;
    clrscr();  // Clears the console screen
    printf("Press any key: ");
    ch = getch();  // Waits for key press
    printf("You pressed: ");
    putchar(ch);  // Display the pressed key
    return 0;
}
```

Note: The use of `conio.h` is deprecated and not part of the standard C library. It is supported by certain compilers like Turbo C++ but is not available in modern environments like GCC or Clang.

---

4. `stdlib.h` (Standard Library)

- **Purpose:** Provides functions for performing general utilities such as memory allocation, process control, conversions, and others.
- **Functions:**
  - `malloc()`: Allocates memory dynamically.
  - `free()`: Frees dynamically allocated memory.
  - `exit()`: Terminates the program.
  - `atoi()`: Converts a string to an integer.
  - `atof()`: Converts a string to a floating-point number.

Example:

```
#include <stdlib.h>

int main() {
    int *ptr;
    ptr = (int *)malloc(sizeof(int));   // Dynamically allocate memory
    *ptr = 10;   // Assign value
    printf("Value: %d\n", *ptr);
    free(ptr);   // Free allocated memory
    return 0;
}
```

5. `string.h` (String Manipulation)

- **Purpose:** Provides functions to manipulate C-style strings (arrays of characters).
- **Functions:**
  - `strlen()`: Returns the length of a string.
  - `strcpy()`: Copies one string to another.
  - `strcmp()`: Compares two strings.
  - `strcat()`: Concatenates two strings.
  - `strchr()`: Finds the first occurrence of a character in a string.

Example:

```
#include <string.h>

int main() {
    char str1[] = "Hello, ";
    char str2[] = "World!";
    strcat(str1, str2);   // Concatenate str2 to str1
    printf("Combined string: %s\n", str1);
    return 0;
}
```

6. `math.h` (Mathematical Operations)

- **Purpose:** Provides functions for basic mathematical operations.
- **Functions:**
  - `sqrt()`: Returns the square root of a number.
  - `pow()`: Raises a number to the power of another number.
  - `sin()`, `cos()`, `tan()`: Trigonometric functions.
  - `log()`: Returns the logarithm of a number.

Example:

```
#include <math.h>

int main() {
    double result = sqrt(25);   // Find the square root of 25
    printf("Square root of 25 is: %.2f\n", result);
    return 0;
}
```

7. `time.h` (Time and Date)

- **Purpose:** Provides functions to manipulate date and time.
- **Functions:**
  - `time()`: Returns the current system time.
  - `localtime()`: Converts time to local time.
  - `strftime()`: Formats time into a human-readable string.

Example:

```
#include <time.h>

int main() {
    time_t t;
    time(&t);   // Get current time
    printf("Current time: %s", ctime(&t));
    return 0;
}
```

Summary of Key Header Files:

1. `stdio.h` - For standard input and output operations.
2. `iostream.h` - For stream-based I/O in C++ (use `<iostream>` in modern C++).
3. `conio.h` - Console I/O (often deprecated and compiler-specific).
4. `stdlib.h` - For memory allocation, process control, and conversions.
5. `string.h` - For string manipulation.
6. `math.h` - For mathematical operations.
7. `time.h` - For time and date manipulation

Practical Examples with Solutions and Output

1. Variable Declaration and Initialization (C++)

```
#include <iostream>
using namespace std;

int main() {
    int num = 10;
    float pi = 3.14;
    cout << "Number: " << num << ", Pi: " << pi << endl;
    return 0;
}
```

Output:

```
Number: 10, Pi: 3.14
```

2. Arithmetic and Logical Operators (C++)

```
#include <iostream>
using namespace std;

int main() {
    int a = 5, b = 10;
    cout << "Sum: " << (a + b) << endl;
    cout << "Logical AND: " << (a > 0 && b > 0) << endl;
    return 0;
}
```

Output:

```
Sum: 15
Logical AND: 1
```

3. Type Casting (C++)

```cpp
#include <iostream>
using namespace std;

int main() {
    int num = 5;
    float result = (float)num / 2;
    cout << "Result: " << result << endl;
    return 0;}
```

Output:

```
Result: 2.5
```

4. Using `getchar()` and `putchar()` (C++)

In C++, it's better to use `cin` and `cout`, but if you want to use `getchar()` and `putchar()`, here's how it would look:

```cpp
#include <iostream>
using namespace std;

int main() {
    char ch;
    cout << "Enter a character: ";
    ch = getchar();
    cout << "You entered: ";
    putchar(ch);
    return 0;
}
```

Output:

```
Enter a character: A
You entered: A
```

5. Formatted I/O (C++)

```cpp
#include <iostream>
using namespace std;

int main() {
    int num;
    cout << "Enter a number: ";
    cin >> num;
    cout << "You entered: " << num << endl;
    return 0;
}
```

Output:

```
Enter a number: 15
You entered: 15
```

25 MCQ ON THESE TOPICS

1. Declaring, Defining, and Initializing Variables

1. Which of the following is a valid variable declaration in C++?
    a) int 1var;
    b) int var_1;
    c) int var-1;
    d) int #var;
    Answer: b
2. What is the correct way to initialize an integer variable in C++?
    a) int x = 0;
    b) int x(0);
    c) Both a and b
    d) None of the above
    Answer: c
3. Which of the following is not a valid identifier in C++?
    a) _temp
    b) 2ndValue
    c) value_2
    d) ValueTwo
    Answer: b

2. Scope of Variables and Named Constants

4. Variables declared inside a function are called:
    a) Global variables
    b) Local variables
    c) Static variables
    d) None of the above
    Answer: b
5. Which keyword is used to declare a constant in C++?
    a) define
    b) const
    c) static
    d) final
    Answer: b
6. What is the scope of a global variable?
    a) Within the function
    b) Throughout the program

c) Within a block
d) None of the above
Answer: b

---

3. Keywords and Data Types

7. Which of the following is not a valid C++ keyword?
   a) for
   b) int
   c) mutable
   d) main
   Answer: d
8. The data type used to store true/false values in C++ is:
   a) bool
   b) int
   c) char
   d) void
   Answer: a
9. What is the size of the `int` data type in most modern compilers?
   a) 1 byte
   b) 2 bytes
   c) 4 bytes
   d) 8 bytes
   Answer: c

---

4. Casting of Data Types

10. Converting a `float` to an `int` in C++ is an example of:
    a) Implicit casting
    b) Explicit casting
    c) Type coercion
    d) None of the above
    Answer: b
11. What is the syntax for casting an `int` to a `float` in C++?
    a) (float) intVar
    b) float(intVar)
    c) Both a and b
    d) None of the above
    Answer: c
12. Which type of casting is performed automatically by the compiler?
    a) Explicit casting
    b) Implicit casting

c) Static casting
d) Dynamic casting
Answer: b

5. Operators: Arithmetic, Logical, and Bitwise

13. Which of the following is not an arithmetic operator in C++?
    a) +
    b) -
    c) &
    d) /
    Answer: c
14. What does the `&&` operator do in C++?
    a) Bitwise AND
    b) Logical AND
    c) Logical OR
    d) Bitwise OR
    Answer: b
15. Which operator is used for bitwise OR?
    a) &&
    b) ||
    c) |
    d) ^
    Answer: c

6. Using Comments in Programs

16. What is the correct syntax for a single-line comment in C++?
    a) // Comment
    b) /* Comment */
    c) # Comment
    d) None of the above
    Answer: a
17. What is the correct syntax for a multi-line comment in C++?
    a) // Comment
    b) /* Comment */
    c) # Comment
    d) None of the above
    Answer: b

7. Character I/O (getc, getchar, putc, putchar)

18. Which function is used to read a single character from the console in C?
    a) getchar()
    b) putchar()
    c) getc()
    d) printf()
    Answer: a

19. Which function writes a character to the console in C?
    a) putchar()
    b) printf()
    c) getc()
    d) getchar()
    Answer: a

20. What is the difference between `getc()` and `getchar()`?
    a) `getc()` is faster than `getchar()`
    b) `getc()` requires a file pointer, while `getchar()` does not
    c) `getchar()` is for files, and `getc()` is for console
    d) None of the above
    Answer: b

8. Formatted and Console I/O (printf(), scanf(), cin, cout)

21. What is the correct syntax for printing a formatted string in C?
    a) printf("Hello, %s", name);
    b) cout << "Hello, " << name;
    c) print("Hello, %s", name);
    d) write("Hello, %s", name);
    Answer: a

22. How do you read input using `cin` in C++?
    a) cin << variable;
    b) cin >> variable;
    c) scanf("%d", &variable);
    d) input(variable);
    Answer: b

23. Which function is used to format input in C++?
    a) scanf()
    b) printf()
    c) cin
    d) cout
    Answer: a

9. Basic Header Files: stdio.h, iostream.h, conio.h

24. Which header file is used for basic input/output functions in C++?
    a) stdio.h
    b) iostream.h
    c) conio.h
    d) string.h
    Answer: b

25. The function `clrscr()` is defined in which header file?
    a) stdio.h
    b) conio.h
    c) iostream.h
    d) math.h
    Answer: b

CHAPTER-3

CONDITIONAL STATEMENTS: IF AND SWITCH-CASE CONSTRUCTS

if Statement in C++:

```cpp
#include <iostream>
using namespace std;

int main() {
    int age = 18;
    if (age >= 18) {
        cout << "You are eligible to vote." << endl;
    }
    return 0;
}
```

Explanation: The condition age >= 18 is true, so the message "You are eligible to vote." is printed.

if-else Statement in C++:

```cpp
#include <iostream>
using namespace std;

int main() {
    int age = 16;
    if (age >= 18) {
        cout << "You are eligible to vote." << endl;
    } else {
        cout << "You are not eligible to vote." << endl;
    }
    return 0;
}
```

Explanation: The condition age >= 18 is false (since age = 16), so the message "You are not eligible to vote." is printed.

switch-case Statement in C++:

```cpp
#include <iostream>
using namespace std;

int main() {
    int day = 3;
    switch (day) {
        case 1:
            cout << "Monday" << endl;
            break;
        case 2:
            cout << "Tuesday" << endl;
```

```
            break;
        case 3:
            cout << "Wednesday" << endl;
            break;
        default:
            cout << "Invalid day" << endl;
    }
    return 0;
}
```

Explanation: The variable `day` is equal to 3, so the code inside `case 3` is executed, and the message "Wednesday" is printed.

Nested Conditional Statements in C++:

```
#include <iostream>
using namespace std;

int main() {
    int age = 20;
    if (age >= 18) {
        cout << "You are eligible to vote." << endl;
        if (age >= 21) {
            cout << "You can also drink alcohol." << endl;
        }
    } else {
        cout << "You are not eligible to vote." << endl;
    }
    return 0;
}
```

Explanation: Since `age = 20`, the first condition `age >= 18` is true, so "You are eligible to vote." is printed. The nested `if` checks if `age >= 21`, but since it is false, "You can also drink alcohol." is not printed.

1. while Loop in C++:

```
#include <iostream>
using namespace std;

int main() {
    int i = 0;
    while (i < 5) {
        cout << i << " ";
        i++;
    }
    return 0;
}
```

Explanation: The loop will print numbers from 0 to 4. It continues until i reaches 5, and i++ increments i by 1 after each iteration.

2. do-while Loop in C++:

```cpp
#include <iostream>
using namespace std;

int main() {
    int i = 0;
    do {
        cout << i << " ";
        i++;
    } while (i < 5);
    return 0;
}
```

Explanation: Similar to the while loop, but in the do-while loop, the code block runs at least once, even if the condition is false initially. It prints numbers from 0 to 4.

3. for Loop in C++:

```cpp
#include <iostream>
using namespace std;

int main() {
    for (int i = 0; i < 5; i++) {
        cout << i << " ";
    }
    return 0;
}
```

Explanation: The for loop starts with i = 0, and increments i until it reaches 5. It prints numbers from 0 to 4.

Key Differences Between Loops in C++:

Aspect	while loop	do-while loop	for loop
Condition check	Before entering the loop	After entering the loop	Before each iteration
Guaranteed execution	No, if condition is false initially	Yes, executes at least once	Yes, based on initialization and condition
Use case	When the number of iterations is unknown	When the loop must run at least once	When the number of iterations is known beforehand

Using break and continue in Loops:

Example using break:

```cpp
#include <iostream>
using namespace std;

int main() {
    for (int i = 0; i < 5; i++) {
        if (i == 3) {
            break;  // Exits the loop when i is 3
        }
        cout << i << " ";
    }
    return 0;
}
```

Output: 0 1 2

Explanation: The break statement exits the loop when i becomes 3, so the loop does not print 3 and stops after printing 0, 1, and 2.

Example using continue:

```cpp
#include <iostream>
using namespace std;

int main() {
    for (int i = 0; i < 5; i++) {
        if (i == 3) {
            continue;  // Skips this iteration when i is 3
        }
        cout << i << " ";
    }
    return 0;
}
```

Output: 0 1 2 4

Explanation: The continue statement skips the iteration where i is 3, so it is not printed, but the loop continues and prints 0, 1, 2, and 4.

Nested Loops in C++:

```cpp
#include <iostream>
using namespace std;

int main() {
    for (int i = 0; i < 3; i++) {
        for (int j = 0; j < 2; j++) {
            cout << "i = " << i << ", j = " << j << endl;
        }
    }
    return 0;}
```

Output:

```
i = 0, j = 0

i = 0, j = 1
i = 1, j = 0
i = 1, j = 1
i = 2, j = 0
i = 2, j = 1
```

Explanation: The outer `for` loop runs 3 times (for `i` = 0, 1, 2), and for each iteration, the inner loop runs 2 times (for `j` = 0, 1), printing the values of `i` and `j` for each combination.

---

4. Use of break and continue in Loops

Both `break` and `continue` are control statements that allow for more flexible behavior inside loops. Here's an explanation of each, along with examples.

---

1. break Statement in C++:

The `break` statement is used to immediately exit a loop or a `switch` statement, regardless of whether the loop's condition is true or not. It helps terminate the loop early.

Syntax:

```
break;
```

- The loop stops execution when `break` is encountered, and the program continues with the statement immediately following the loop.

Example:

```cpp
#include <iostream>
using namespace std;

int main() {
    for (int i = 0; i < 10; i++) {
        if (i == 5) {
            break;   // Exit the loop when i equals 5
        }
        cout << i << " ";
    }
    // Output: 0 1 2 3 4
    return 0;
}
```

Explanation:

- When i becomes 5, the `break` statement is triggered, causing the loop to exit immediately. The output prints the numbers 0 to 4 before breaking out of the loop.

2. continue Statement in C++:

The `continue` statement is used to skip the current iteration of the loop and proceed with the next iteration. It does not exit the loop but instead jumps to the next iteration, re-evaluating the condition.

Syntax:

```
continue;
```

- When `continue` is encountered, the remaining code in the loop for that iteration is skipped, and the loop continues with the next iteration.

Example:

```cpp
#include <iostream>
using namespace std;

int main() {
    for (int i = 0; i < 5; i++) {
        if (i == 3) {
            continue;   // Skip iteration when i equals 3
        }
        cout << i << " ";
    }
    // Output: 0 1 2 4
    return 0;
}
```

Explanation:

- When i is equal to 3, the `continue` statement is triggered, and the loop skips printing 3. The loop prints 0, 1, 2, and 4, skipping the iteration where i equals 3.

Key Differences Between `break` and `continue`:

Statement	Purpose	Effect	Behavior
break	Exit the loop completely.	Exits the loop entirely, skipping any remaining iterations.	The program continues with the first statement after the loop.
continue	Skip the current iteration.	Skips the remaining code in the current iteration and moves to the next iteration.	The loop continues to the next iteration after re-checking the condition.

3. Example with Both `break` and `continue`:

Example:

```cpp
#include <iostream>
using namespace std;

int main() {
    for (int i = 0; i < 10; i++) {
        if (i == 3) {
            continue;  // Skip iteration when i equals 3
        }
        if (i == 7) {
            break;  // Exit the loop when i equals 7
        }
        cout << i << " ";
    }
    // Output: 0 1 2 4 5 6
    return 0;
}
```

Explanation:

- When i == 3, the `continue` statement skips printing 3 and proceeds to the next iteration.
- When i == 7, the `break` statement exits the loop before 7 is printed. Hence, the output will print 0 1 2 4 5 6 and then break out of the loop.

4. Nested Conditional Statements in C++:

A nested conditional statement is when an `if` or `switch` statement is placed inside another `if` or `switch` statement. This allows for more complex decision-making, as multiple conditions can be checked in a hierarchical manner.

Example:

```cpp
#include <iostream>
using namespace std;

int main() {
    int age = 20;
    int hasVoterID = 1;

    if (age >= 18) {
        if (hasVoterID) {
            cout << "You can vote." << endl;
        } else {
            cout << "You need a Voter ID." << endl;
        }
    } else {
        cout << "You are not eligible to vote." << endl;
    }
    // Output: You can vote.
    return 0;
}
```

Explanation:

- The outer `if` checks if the person is eligible to vote based on age.
- The inner `if` checks whether the person has a Voter ID.
- If the person is of voting age but does not have a Voter ID, they are informed about the need for one. If the person is under 18, they are informed that they are not eligible to vote.

5. Nested Loops in C++:

A nested loop is when one loop is placed inside another. It allows you to perform repeated operations within another set of repeated operations, which is useful for multi-dimensional problems like matrices.

Example:

```cpp
#include <iostream>
using namespace std;

int main() {
    for (int i = 0; i < 3; i++) {
        for (int j = 0; j < 3; j++) {
            cout << "i = " << i << ", j = " << j << endl;
        }
```

```
    }
    // Output:
    // i = 0, j = 0
    // i = 0, j = 1
    // i = 0, j = 2
    // i = 1, j = 0
    // i = 1, j = 1
    // i = 1, j = 2
    // i = 2, j = 0
    // i = 2, j = 1
    // i = 2, j = 2
    return 0;
}
```

Explanation:

- The outer `for` loop runs from `i = 0` to `i = 2`.
- For each iteration of the outer loop, the inner `for` loop runs from `j = 0` to `j = 2`.
- The result is that all combinations of `i` and `j` are printed.

Key Points About Nested Conditional and Iterative Statements:

1. **Readability:** While nested conditionals and loops are useful, excessive nesting can make code harder to read. Aim for simplicity and clarity.
2. **Complexity:** Nested loops can increase the time complexity of an algorithm. For example, a nested loop that runs n times inside another n times will have a time complexity of $O(n^2)$.
3. **Practical Use:**
   - Nested conditionals are used in situations like decision trees, where different actions are performed based on multiple conditions.
   - Nested loops are commonly used when working with multi-dimensional data structures, such as 2D arrays or matrices.

6. Example of Complex Nested Statements in C++:

Example:

```
#include <iostream>
using namespace std;

int main() {
    for (int i = 0; i < 3; i++) {
        for (int j = 0; j < 3; j++) {
            if (i == j) {
                cout << "i and j are equal: i = " << i << ", j = " << j <<
endl;
            } else {
                cout << "i and j are not equal: i = " << i << ", j = " <<
j << endl;
            }
```

```
        }
    }
    // Output:
    // i and j are equal: i = 0, j = 0
    // i and j are not equal: i = 0, j = 1
    // i and j are not equal: i = 0, j = 2
    // i and j are not equal: i = 1, j = 0
    // i and j are equal: i = 1, j = 1
    // i and j are not equal: i = 1, j = 2
    // i and j are not equal: i = 2, j = 0
    // i and j are not equal: i = 2, j = 1
    // i and j are equal: i = 2, j = 2
    return 0;
}
```

Explanation:

- This example uses nested loops combined with an `if-else` condition.
- It checks whether `i` and `j` are equal and prints appropriate messages based on the result.

25 MCQ ON THESE TOPICS

1. Simple Expressions and Operator Precedence

1. Which operator has the highest precedence in C++?
   a) +
   b) *
   c) ()
   d) =
   Answer: c

2. What is the output of the following expression:
   `int x = 5; int y = 2; cout << x / y;`
   a) 2.5
   b) 2
   c) 3
   d) 2.0
   Answer: b

3. In the expression `a + b * c`, which operation is performed first?
   a) Addition
   b) Multiplication
   c) Both are performed simultaneously
   d) None of the above
   Answer: b

4. What is the associativity of the assignment operator = in C++?
   a) Left-to-right
   b) Right-to-left
   c) Depends on the context
   d) None of the above
   Answer: b

5. Which of the following is not a valid expression?
   a) a + (b * c)
   b) (a + b) *
   c) a + b * c
   d) a * (b + c)
   Answer: b

2. Conditional Statements: if and switch-case Constructs

6. What is the correct syntax for an `if` statement in C++?
   a) if condition then statement;
   b) if (condition) statement;
   c) if (condition) { statement }
   d) Both b and c
   Answer: d

7. What will be the output of the following code?

```
int x = 10;
if (x > 5)
    cout << "True";
else
    cout << "False";
```

   a) True
   b) False
   c) No output
   d) Compilation error
   Answer: a

8. In a `switch` statement, each `case` must end with:
   a) break
   b) continue
   c) return
   d) None of the above
   Answer: a

9. What happens if there is no `break` in a `switch` case?
   a) The program exits the `switch` immediately
   b) All subsequent cases are executed until a `break` is found
   c) Only the default case is executed
   d) The program throws an error
   Answer: b

10. Which of the following is not allowed in a `switch` statement?
    a) char
    b) float
    c) int

d) enum
Answer: b

---

3. Iterative Statements: while, do-while, and for Loops

11. Which loop is guaranteed to execute at least once?
    a) for
    b) while
    c) do-while
    d) None of the above
    Answer: c

12. What is the correct syntax for a `for` loop in C++?
    a) for (initialization; condition; update) { statement; }
    b) for initialization; condition; update { statement; }
    c) for { initialization; condition; update }
    d) None of the above
    Answer: a

13. What will be the output of the following code?

```cpp
int x = 1;
while (x < 5) {
    cout << x << " ";
    x++;
}
```

    a) 1 2 3 4
    b) 1 2 3 4 5
    c) Infinite loop
    d) No output
    Answer: a

14. Which of the following is correct about the `do-while` loop?
    a) The condition is checked before executing the loop body
    b) The condition is checked after executing the loop body
    c) It executes at least two times
    d) None of the above
    Answer: b

15. What will be the output of the following code?

```cpp
int x = 0;
for (; x < 3;) {
    cout << x;
    x++;
}
```

a) 012
b) 123
c) 01
d) Compilation error
Answer: a

---

4. Use of break and continue in Loops

16. What does the `break` statement do in a loop?
    a) Terminates the loop and transfers control to the next statement
    b) Skips the current iteration
    c) Repeats the loop
    d) None of the above
    Answer: a

17. What does the `continue` statement do in a loop?
    a) Terminates the loop
    b) Skips the rest of the loop body for the current iteration
    c) Ends the program
    d) None of the above
    Answer: b

18. What will be the output of the following code?

```
for (int i = 0; i < 5; i++) {
    if (i == 3) continue;
    cout << i << " ";
}
```

    a) 0 1 2 3 4
    b) 0 1 2 4
    c) 1 2 4
    d) Compilation error
    Answer: b

19. In which type of loops can the `break` statement be used?
    a) for
    b) while
    c) do-while
    d) All of the above
    Answer: d

20. In which type of loops can the `continue` statement be used?
    a) for
    b) while
    c) do-while
    d) All of the above
    Answer: d

5. Nested Conditional and Iterative Statements

21. Which of the following is correct for nested loops?
    a) A loop inside another loop
    b) A loop with multiple conditions
    c) A loop with no condition
    d) None of the above
    Answer: a

22. How many times will the inner loop execute in the following code?

```
for (int i = 0; i < 3; i++) {
    for (int j = 0; j < 2; j++) {
        cout << "*";
    } }
```

    a) 3
    b) 6
    c) 5
    d) 2
    Answer: b

23. Can `if` statements be nested within loops?
    a) Yes, always
    b) No, it is not allowed
    c) Only in `for` loops
    d) Only in `while` loops
    Answer: a

24. Which of the following is valid for nested loops?
    a) for inside for
    b) while inside for
    c) do-while inside for
    d) All of the above
    Answer: d

25. What will be the output of the following code?

```
for (int i = 1; i <= 2; i++) {
    for (int j = 1; j <= 2; j++) {
        if (i == j) break;
        cout << i << j << " ";
    }
}
```

    a) 12 21
    b) 21
    c) 11 22
    d) None of the above
    Answer: b

CHAPTER-4

FUNCTIONS AND ARRAYS

Utility and Types of Functions (Call by Value and Call by Reference)

Functions in C allow us to divide the program into smaller, manageable blocks of code that perform specific tasks. This helps in improving readability, reusability, and maintainability of code.

1. Call by Value:

In Call by Value, a copy of the actual value of the argument is passed to the function. The parameter inside the function holds the copy of the value, and any changes made to the parameter do not affect the original variable.

```cpp
#include <iostream>
using namespace std;

void add(int a, int b) {
    a = a + b; // Changes are local to the function
    cout << "Inside function: " << a << endl;
}

int main() {
    int x = 5, y = 10;
    add(x, y);   // x and y are passed by value
    cout << "In main: x = " << x << endl; // x remains unchanged
    return 0;
}
```

Output:

```
Inside function: 15
In main: x = 5
```

2. Call by Reference:

In Call by Reference, the address (reference) of the argument is passed to the function. This allows the function to modify the actual variable, as it has access to the memory location of the argument.

```cpp
#include <iostream>
using namespace std;

void add(int* a, int* b) {
    *a = *a + *b; // Modifies the original value using pointers
```

```
        cout << "Inside function: " << *a << endl;
}

int main() {
    int x = 5, y = 10;
    add(&x, &y); // Pass the address of x and y
    cout << "In main: x = " << x << endl; // x is modified
    return 0; }
```

Output:

```
Inside function: 15
In main: x = 15
```

Key Differences between Call by Value and Call by Reference:

Aspect	Call by Value	Call by Reference
Argument Passing	Passes a copy of the value to the function.	Passes the memory address (reference) of the argument.
Effect on Original Data	Does not affect the original variable.	Modifies the original variable.
Usage	Safer for simple operations where the original value shouldn't change.	Useful when we need to modify the original values.
Performance	Slightly slower for large data as the entire copy of the data is passed.	More efficient for large data, as only the address is passed.

3. Functions Returning Value and void Functions:

Functions Returning Value:

Functions that return a value perform some operations and return a result to the caller using the `return` statement.

```
#include <iostream>
using namespace std;

int add(int a, int b) {
    return a + b;  // Returns the result to the caller
}

int main() {
    int result = add(5, 10);  // Calls the add function and stores the
result
    cout << "Sum: " << result << endl;  // Prints the result
```

```
    return 0;
}
```

Output:

```
Sum: 15
```

void Functions:

A void function does not return a value. These functions are typically used when the function is meant to perform an action but does not need to send any result back to the caller.

```
#include <iostream>
using namespace std;

void printMessage() {
    cout << "This is a void function." << endl;
}

int main() {
    printMessage();  // Calls the void function
    return 0;
}
```

Output:

```
This is a void function.
```

Key Differences between Functions Returning Value and void Functions:

Aspect	Functions Returning Value	void Functions
Return Type	Specifies a return type (e.g., int, float).	Return type is void, meaning no value is returned.
Purpose	Used when the function needs to return a result to the caller.	Used when the function performs an action but doesn't return any result.
Usage	Useful for calculations or processing that produces a value.	Useful for performing actions like printing, modifying global variables, etc.
Example	`int add(int a, int b) { return a + b; }`	`void printMessage() { cout << "Hello!"; }`

Summary:

- **Call by Value** is used when you do not want the original variable to be modified.
- **Call by Reference** is used when changes in the function need to reflect on the original variable.

- **Functions Returning Value** are used when you need to send a result back from the function.
- **void Functions** are used for actions that do not require returning any value.

---

3. Inline Functions and Function Parameters

An **inline function** in C++ is a function where the compiler attempts to insert the function's code directly at the point where the function is called, instead of performing the regular function call mechanism, which involves a jump to the function code and a return.

Using **inline functions** can help to eliminate the overhead of function calls, especially for small functions, thus improving performance. The `inline` keyword tells the compiler to insert the function's body wherever the function is called, but it is important to note that this is only a suggestion, and the compiler may choose not to inline the function if it deems it inefficient or too large.

Syntax of Inline Function in C++:
```
inline return_type function_name(parameters) {
    // Function body
}
```
Example of Inline Function:
```
#include <iostream>
using namespace std;

inline int add(int a, int b) {
    return a + b;   // Inline function to add two numbers
}

int main() {
    int result = add(5, 10);   // Function call
    cout << "Sum: " << result << endl;   // Output the result
    return 0;
}
```

Output:

```
Sum: 15
```

In the above example:

- The function `add()` is marked as `inline`.
- Instead of a traditional function call, the compiler attempts to insert the expression `a + b` directly at the call location in `main()`.
- The result of `add(5, 10)` is computed directly and stored in the variable `result`, which is then printed.

- **Small Functions**: Inline functions are typically used for small functions that are called frequently. Functions like adding two numbers, returning the square of a number, or other simple operations are ideal candidates for inlining.
- **Performance Optimization**: They are used to avoid the overhead of function calls in performance-critical code.

Limitations of Inline Functions:

- **Size of Function**: If the function is too large, inlining it may actually degrade performance. For example, if the function contains loops, complex logic, or recursion, the compiler may ignore the inline suggestion.
- **Recursive Functions**: Recursive functions cannot be inlined because they call themselves.

Function Parameters in C++:

In C++, function parameters can be passed either **by value** or **by reference**.

1. **Call by Value**: A copy of the argument is passed to the function. Any modifications made to the parameter inside the function do not affect the original argument.
2. **Call by Reference**: The address (reference) of the argument is passed. Changes made to the parameter inside the function will affect the original argument.

C++ also supports **default parameters**. Default parameters are values that the function parameters take if no argument is provided when the function is called.

Example of Function Parameters (Call by Value and Call by Reference):

```
#include <iostream>
using namespace std;

// Call by Value: The argument value is copied to the parameter
void addByValue(int a, int b) {
    a = a + b;   // Changes to 'a' won't affect the original argument
    cout << "Inside addByValue: " << a << endl;
}

// Call by Reference: The reference (address) of the argument is passed
void addByReference(int &a, int &b) {
    a = a + b;   // Changes to 'a' will affect the original argument
    cout << "Inside addByReference: " << a << endl;
}

int main() {
    int x = 5, y = 10;

    // Call by Value
    addByValue(x, y);   // x remains unchanged
```

```
    cout << "After addByValue, x = " << x << endl;   // x remains 5

    // Call by Reference
    addByReference(x, y);   // x is modified
    cout << "After addByReference, x = " << x << endl;   // x is now 15

    return 0;
}
```

Output:

```
Inside addByValue: 15
After addByValue, x = 5
Inside addByReference: 15
After addByReference, x = 15
```

In this example:

- **Call by Value** (addByValue) creates a copy of x and y inside the function, so the original values of x and y in main() remain unchanged.
- **Call by Reference** (addByReference) uses references (addresses) of x and y, so any change made inside the function reflects in the original variables.

Default Parameters in C++:

C++ allows you to provide default values for function parameters. If no argument is passed for a parameter, the default value is used.

```
#include <iostream>
using namespace std;

void greet(string name = "Guest") {
    cout << "Hello, " << name << "!" << endl;
}

int main() {
    greet("Alice");   // Passes "Alice"
    greet();   // Uses default "Guest"
    return 0;
}
```

Output:

```
Hello, Alice!
Hello, Guest!
```

Here, the function greet() has a default parameter name = "Guest". When no argument is provided in the second call (greet()), the default value "Guest" is used.

Key Takeaways:

1. **Inline Functions**:
   - ○ Helps to reduce function call overhead.
   - ○ Ideal for small functions.
   - ○ The compiler may ignore the inline suggestion for larger or complex functions.
2. **Function Parameters**:
   - ○ **Call by Value**: A copy of the argument is passed.
   - ○ **Call by Reference**: The address of the argument is passed.
   - ○ **Default Parameters**: Allows functions to use default values for parameters if none is passed.
3. **Use Cases**:
   - ○ Inline functions are used for performance-critical, simple functions.
   - ○ Call by reference is used when you want to modify the actual argument.
   - ○ Default parameters provide flexibility in function calls.

---

4. Command Line Arguments in Functions:

Command-line arguments allow you to pass values to the program when running it from the command line. These are received as arguments in the `main` function.

Syntax:
```
int main(int argc, char *argv[]) { ... }
```

- **argc** represents the number of arguments.
- **argv[]** is an array of strings that hold the arguments passed.

Example:
```cpp
#include <iostream>
using namespace std;

int main(int argc, char *argv[]) {
    cout << "Number of arguments: " << argc << endl;
    for (int i = 0; i < argc; i++) {
        cout << "Argument " << i << ": " << argv[i] << endl;
    }
    return 0;
}
```

Command Line Input:

```
./a.out Hello World
```

Output:

```
Number of arguments: 3
Argument 0: ./a.out
```

```
Argument 1: Hello
Argument 2: World
```

5. One-Dimensional Arrays (Declaring, Initializing, and Manipulating Elements):

Declaring Arrays:

An array in C++ is a collection of elements that are of the same data type, stored in contiguous memory locations. The syntax for declaring an array is:

```
data_type array_name[size];
```

Here, `data_type` is the type of the elements (e.g., `int`, `float`, `char`), `array_name` is the name of the array, and `size` is the number of elements in the array.

Example:

```
int arr[5]; // Declaring an integer array of size 5
```

This declares an array `arr` that can store 5 integer values. The values in the array are uninitialized initially (they may contain garbage values until you explicitly assign values to them).

Initializing Arrays:

Arrays can be initialized either at the time of declaration or later in the code. The initialization assigns values to the elements of the array.

- **At the time of declaration:** You can initialize an array at the moment of declaration by providing values inside curly braces `{}`.

  Example:

  ```
  int arr[5] = {1, 2, 3, 4, 5}; // Initializing an integer array with
  5 elements
  ```

  This array has 5 elements, and each element is assigned a value from the initializer list.

- **Partial Initialization:** If you provide fewer values than the size of the array, the remaining elements are automatically initialized to zero.

  Example:

int `arr[5] = {1, 2};` // Initializes arr[0] = 1, arr[1] = 2, and arr[2], arr[3], arr[4] = 0

- **If you don't initialize the array, the elements will contain garbage values (unpredictable values).**

Manipulating Array Elements:

Array elements are accessed using their index. In C++, the indices of an array start from 0. You can manipulate array elements by accessing them through their index.

Example:

```cpp
#include <iostream>
using namespace std;

int main() {
    int arr[5] = {1, 2, 3, 4, 5}; // Initializing an array with 5 elements

    // Accessing the first element (arr[0])
    cout << "First element: " << arr[0] << endl; // Output: 1

    // Modifying the third element (arr[2])
    arr[2] = 10; // arr[2] is modified from 3 to 10

    // Printing the modified third element
    cout << "Modified third element: " << arr[2] << endl; // Output: 10

    return 0;
}
```

Output:

```
First element: 1
Modified third element: 10
```

- **Accessing Array Elements:** In this code, `arr[0]` accesses the first element of the array, and `arr[2]` accesses the third element.
- **Modifying Array Elements:** You can modify the value of any element in the array using its index. In the example, `arr[2] = 10;` changes the value of the third element from 3 to 10.

Summary:

- **Declaring Arrays:** Arrays are declared with a specified size and type. The elements of an array are stored in contiguous memory locations.
- **Initializing Arrays:** Arrays can be initialized with values at the time of declaration. If fewer values are provided, the remaining elements are set to 0. If no values are provided, the elements may contain garbage values.

- **Manipulating Array Elements:** You can access and modify array elements using indices. The index starts from `0` and goes up to `size-1`.

---

6. Working with Strings and Various Data Types in Arrays

Strings in Arrays:

In C++, strings are often represented as arrays of characters. A string is essentially a sequence of characters terminated by a null character (`\0`), which marks the end of the string.

Example:

```cpp
#include <iostream>
using namespace std;

int main() {
    char str[] = "Hello"; // String in array form
    cout << "String: " << str << endl;
    return 0;
}
```

Output:

```
String: Hello
```

- The string `"Hello"` is stored as an array of characters, and the null character `\0` is automatically appended at the end of the string to indicate the end.
- In this case, the array `str` will contain the characters `{'H', 'e', 'l', 'l', 'o', '\0'}`.

Arrays with Different Data Types:

In C++, you can create arrays that hold various data types, such as integers, floating-point numbers, or characters. Each type of array will store elements of the corresponding data type.

Examples:

- **Integer Array:**

  ```cpp
  int arr[3] = {1, 2, 3}; // Array of integers
  ```

- **Float Array:**

  ```cpp
  float f_arr[2] = {1.5, 2.5}; // Array of floats
  ```

- **Character Array:**

```cpp
char c_arr[3] = {'A', 'B', 'C'}; // Array of characters
```

In all cases, each array will contain elements of the respective data type and can be accessed and manipulated in a similar manner.

Summary of Key Concepts:

- **Strings in Arrays:** In C++, strings are stored as arrays of characters, and the null character \0 marks the end of the string.
- **Arrays with Different Data Types:** Arrays can store different types of data, such as integers, floats, and characters. You can create arrays for each of these data types and manipulate them similarly.

Two-Dimensional Arrays (Rows and Columns)

7. Two-Dimensional Arrays (Rows and Columns)

A **two-dimensional array** in C++ can be considered as an array of arrays. It is used to store data in a table-like structure with rows and columns. Each element in the two-dimensional array is accessed using two indices: one for the row and one for the column.

Syntax:
```cpp
data_type array_name[row_size][column_size];
```

- **data_type**: Specifies the type of elements stored in the array (e.g., int, float, char).
- **array_name**: The name of the array.
- **row_size**: The number of rows in the array.
- **column_size**: The number of columns in the array.

In a two-dimensional array, you can think of it as a matrix with multiple rows and columns, where the number of rows and columns must be defined.

Example:
```cpp
#include <iostream>
using namespace std;

int main() {
    // Declaring and initializing a 2D array with 2 rows and 3 columns
    int arr[2][3] = {{1, 2, 3}, {4, 5, 6}};

    // Accessing the element at row 0, column 1
    cout << "Element at [0][1]: " << arr[0][1] << endl; // Output: 2

    return 0;
}
```

Output:

```
Element at [0][1]: 2
```

- In the example above, the array `arr` is a 2x3 matrix (2 rows and 3 columns). The elements of the matrix are as follows:

```
{ {1, 2, 3},
  {4, 5, 6} }
```

- The element at position `[0][1]` is 2 because it is in the first row (0-based indexing) and second column.

Accessing Elements:

- The elements in a two-dimensional array are accessed using the **row index** and **column index**.
    - `arr[row_index][column_index]` is the syntax to access an element.
    - Indices start from 0, so the first row is `arr[0]`, the second row is `arr[1]`, and so on.
    - Similarly, the first column is `arr[i][0]`, the second column is `arr[i][1]`, and so on for all rows `i`.

Modifying Elements:

You can modify an element in a two-dimensional array by using the same index-based approach:

```
arr[1][2] = 10; // Modify the element at row 1, column 2 to 10
```

8. Introduction to Multi-Dimensional Arrays

In addition to two-dimensional arrays, C++ supports **multi-dimensional arrays**, which have more than two dimensions. These can be used to represent more complex data structures, like 3D arrays (arrays with depth), 4D arrays, and so on.

Example of a 3D Array:

A **three-dimensional array** is essentially an array of two-dimensional arrays, and it can be thought of as a collection of matrices (each with rows and columns).

Syntax:

```
data_type array_name[depth_size][row_size][column_size];
```

- **depth_size**: The number of blocks or layers in the array.

- **`row_size`**: The number of rows in each block.
- **`column_size`**: The number of columns in each row.

Example of Declaring a 3D Array:

```cpp
#include <iostream>
using namespace std;

int main() {
    // Declaring a 3D array with 2 blocks, 3 rows, and 4 columns
    int arr[2][3][4] = {
        {{1, 2, 3, 4}, {5, 6, 7, 8}, {9, 10, 11, 12}},
        {{13, 14, 15, 16}, {17, 18, 19, 20}, {21, 22, 23, 24}}
    };

    // Accessing the element at block 1, row 2, column 3
    cout << "Element at [1][2][3]: " << arr[1][2][3] << endl; // Output:
24

    return 0;
}
```

Output:

```
Element at [1][2][3]: 24
```
Accessing Elements in a 3D Array:

In a 3D array, three indices are used to access an element:

```
arr[block_index][row_index][column_index]
```

For the example above, `arr[1][2][3]` accesses the element in the second block (block 1), third row (row 2), and fourth column (column 3), which is 24.

Example of 3D Array Structure:

The array `arr[2][3][4]` has the following structure:

```
Block 0:
{ {1, 2, 3, 4},
  {5, 6, 7, 8},
  {9, 10, 11, 12} }

Block 1:
{ {13, 14, 15, 16},
  {17, 18, 19, 20},
  {21, 22, 23, 24} }
```

Each block is a 2D array with 3 rows and 4 columns. The indices used to access the elements are `[block][row][column]`.

Just like two-dimensional arrays, you can modify an element in a multi-dimensional array by specifying its indices:

```
arr[1][2][3] = 50; // Modify the element at block 1, row 2, column 3 to 50
```

Summary of Key Concepts:

- **Two-Dimensional Arrays**: A 2D array is an array of arrays, representing data in a table-like format with rows and columns. Elements are accessed using two indices: `[row][column]`.
- **Multi-Dimensional Arrays**: Arrays can have more than two dimensions (e.g., 3D arrays, 4D arrays). These can represent more complex structures like blocks, rows, and columns. Access to elements requires specifying all the indices corresponding to each dimension.

25 MCQ ON THESE TOPICS

1. Utility and Types of Functions (Call by Value and Call by Reference)

1. What is the key difference between "Call by Value" and "Call by Reference"?
   a) Call by value copies the argument, while call by reference uses the actual memory address.
   b) Call by value uses pointers, while call by reference does not.
   c) Call by reference does not allow parameter changes.
   d) There is no difference.
   Answer: a
2. In "Call by Reference," what is passed to the function?
   a) A copy of the variable's value
   b) A reference (memory address) of the variable
   c) A constant value
   d) A pointer to the function
   Answer: b
3. Which of the following is an example of "Call by Value"?
   a) `void func(int &x)`
   b) `void func(int *x)`
   c) `void func(int x)`
   d) None of the above
   Answer: c

4. Which function type allows direct modification of the original argument?
   a) Call by Value
   b) Call by Reference
   c) Both
   d) None
   Answer: b
5. When should "Call by Reference" be preferred over "Call by Value"?
   a) When passing large data structures
   b) When avoiding changes to the actual argument
   c) When using constant values
   d) When debugging
   Answer: a

---

2. Functions Returning Value and void Functions

6. Which of the following correctly declares a function that returns a value?
   a) `void func()`
   b) `int func()`
   c) `void func(int a)`
   d) `float func(int a)`
   Answer: b
7. What is the purpose of a void function?
   a) To return multiple values
   b) To perform actions without returning any value
   c) To allocate memory dynamically
   d) None of the above
   Answer: b
8. Can a void function have parameters?
   a) Yes
   b) No
   c) Only if it's inline
   d) Only with command-line arguments
   Answer: a
9. What will happen if a function does not explicitly return a value, but it is not declared as `void`?
   a) Compilation error
   b) Undefined behavior
   c) Automatically returns 0
   d) Generates a warning
   Answer: a
10. Which keyword is used to return a value from a function?
    a) break
    b) return
    c) continue

d) output
Answer: b

3. Inline Functions and Function Parameters

11. What is the primary advantage of inline functions?
    a) Faster execution by reducing function call overhead
    b) Easier debugging
    c) Reduced memory usage
    d) Allows recursion
    Answer: a
12. Which keyword is used to define an inline function?
    a) inline
    b) function
    c) static
    d) constexpr
    Answer: a
13. Inline functions are generally used for:
    a) Large, complex functions
    b) Small, frequently used functions
    c) Functions with recursion
    d) Functions with global variables
    Answer: b
14. What happens if an inline function contains a loop?
    a) It always gets inlined.
    b) The compiler may choose not to inline it.
    c) Compilation fails.
    d) The loop is executed twice.
    Answer: b
15. Inline functions are expanded at:
    a) Compile time
    b) Runtime
    c) Link time
    d) Execution time
    Answer: a

4. Command Line Arguments in Functions

16. Which of the following is the correct syntax for command-line arguments?
    a) `int main()`
    b) `int main(char* args)`
    c) `int main(int argc, char* argv[])`

d) `int main(int argc, char argv)`
Answer: c

17. What does `argc` represent in the main function?
   a) The number of command-line arguments
   b) The actual arguments passed
   c) The first argument
   d) None of the above
   Answer: a

18. What type is `argv` in the command-line arguments?
   a) Integer
   b) String
   c) Pointer to a char array
   d) None of the above
   Answer: c

19. What is the index of the program name in `argv`?
   a) -1
   b) 0
   c) 1
   d) Depends on the program
   Answer: b

20. How are multiple command-line arguments separated?
   a) By commas
   b) By semicolons
   c) By spaces
   d) By newlines
   Answer: c

5. Arrays and Strings

21. How do you declare a one-dimensional array in C++?
   a) `int arr;`
   b) `int arr[10];`
   c) `arr[10] int;`
   d) `array arr;`
   Answer: b

22. What is the output of the following code?

```cpp
Copy code
int arr[3] = {1, 2, 3};
cout << arr[1];
```

   a) 1
   b) 2
   c) 3

d) Compilation error
Answer: b

23. How is a 2D array declared in C++?
    a) `int arr[3][3];`
    b) `int arr[3,3];`
    c) `array<int, int> arr;`
    d) `int[3][3] arr;`
    Answer: a
24. Which function is used to find the length of a string in C++?
    a) `strlen()`
    b) `size()`
    c) `length()`
    d) Both a and c
    Answer: d
25. What is the index of the first element in a C++ array?
    a) -1
    b) 0
    c) 1
    d) Depends on the compiler
    Answer: b

CHAPTER-5

DERIVED DATA TYPES (STRUCTURES AND UNIONS) IN C++

In C++, **structures** and **unions** are user-defined data types that allow you to group different data types together. Both structures and unions help to create complex data types by combining simple data types. However, the way they store and access data differs significantly.

Structure vs. Union

- **Structure**:
  - A structure is a collection of variables (which can be of different data types) grouped together under a single name.
  - Each member of a structure has its own memory location.
  - The total memory used by a structure is the sum of the memory used by all its members.
  - **Use case**: Structures are used when we need to store multiple pieces of related data, each having its own memory location.
- **Union**:
  - A union is similar to a structure, but all the members of a union share the same memory location.
  - Only one member of the union can hold a value at any given time.
  - The memory size of a union is the size of the largest member, because all members share the same memory.
  - **Use case**: Unions are useful when we need to store different data types, but only one value will be stored at any given time.

Syntax for Structure and Union

1. **Structure Syntax**:

```
struct structure_name {
    data_type member1;
    data_type member2;
    // more members...
};
```

Example of a structure declaration:

```
struct Student {
    int id;
    string name;
```

```
    float grade;};
```

2. **Union Syntax**:

```
union union_name {
    data_type member1;
    data_type member2;
    // more members...
};
```

Example of a union declaration:

```
union Data {
    int intVal;
    float floatVal;
    char charVal;
};
```

Declaring, Initializing, and Using Structures and Unions

1. Structure Declaration and Initialization

To declare and initialize a structure, we define the structure type and then create a variable of that type. We can initialize the structure variables using a list of values.

Example of Declaring and Initializing a Structure:
```cpp
#include <iostream>
using namespace std;

struct Student {
    int id;
    string name;
    float grade;
};

int main() {
    // Initializing a structure variable
    Student student1 = {101, "John", 90.5};

    // Accessing structure members
    cout << "Student ID: " << student1.id << endl;
    cout << "Student Name: " << student1.name << endl;
    cout << "Student Grade: " << student1.grade << endl;

    return 0;
}
```

Output:

```
Student ID: 101
Student Name: John
```

Student Grade: 90.5

In this example:

- We declare a structure `Student` with three members: `id`, `name`, and `grade`.
- We initialize a structure variable `student1` with values `{101, "John", 90.5}`.
- Then, we access the members of the structure using the dot operator (`.`) and print their values.

---

2. Union Declaration and Initialization

In a union, all the members share the same memory location. When a value is assigned to one member, it will overwrite any existing value in the other members.

Example of Declaring and Initializing a Union:

```cpp
#include <iostream>
using namespace std;

union Data {
    int intVal;
    float floatVal;
    char charVal;
};

int main() {
    // Initializing a union variable
    Data data1;
    data1.intVal = 10; // Assigning value to intVal

    // Accessing the union member
    cout << "Integer value: " << data1.intVal << endl;

    data1.floatVal = 3.14; // Assigning value to floatVal
    cout << "Float value: " << data1.floatVal << endl;

    data1.charVal = 'A'; // Assigning value to charVal
    cout << "Char value: " << data1.charVal << endl;

    return 0; }
```

Output:

```
Integer value: 10
Float value: 3.14
Char value: A
```

In this example:

- We define a union `Data` with three members: `intVal`, `floatVal`, and `charVal`.

- We assign values to each member sequentially, but only one value is stored at any time. The last assigned value (`charVal` in this case) is the one that is stored and accessed.

Key Differences Between Structure and Union:

Feature	Structure	Union
Memory Allocation	Each member has its own memory.	All members share the same memory.
Size of the Type	Total size is sum of all members' sizes.	Size is the size of the largest member.
Usage	Used when we need to store multiple related values.	Used when only one value needs to be stored at a time.
Accessing Members	All members can be accessed independently.	Only one member can hold a value at a time.

Summary:

- **Structure**: Used to store multiple values of different data types where each member has its own memory location.
- **Union**: Used when multiple data types are required, but only one of them will hold a value at any given time, and all members share the same memory.

Both structures and unions are essential for creating complex data types in C++, enabling you to group related data together efficiently.

Union Declaration and Initialization in C++

A **union** in C++ is similar to a structure, but it has a key difference: all members of a union share the same memory location. This means that only one member of the union can hold a value at any given time. When a value is assigned to one member, it overwrites the values of the other members.

Syntax for Declaring a Union:

```
union union_name {
    data_type member1;
    data_type member2;
    // more members...};
```

For example:

```
union Data {
    int intVal;
    float floatVal;
    char charVal;};
```

In this example, the `Data` union has three members: `intVal`, `floatVal`, and `charVal`. All these members share the same memory space, meaning the size of the union is determined by the size of its largest member.

Example of Declaring, Initializing, and Using a Union

```cpp
#include <iostream>
using namespace std;

union Data {
    int intVal;
    float floatVal;
    char charVal;
};

int main() {
    // Initializing union variable
    Data data1;

    // Assigning value to intVal
    data1.intVal = 10;
    cout << "Integer value: " << data1.intVal << endl; // Output the
integer value

    // Assigning value to floatVal (this will overwrite intVal)
    data1.floatVal = 3.14;
    cout << "Float value: " << data1.floatVal << endl;  // Output the
float value

    // Assigning value to charVal (this will overwrite floatVal)
    data1.charVal = 'A';
    cout << "Char value: " << data1.charVal << endl;  // Output the char
value

    return 0;
}
```

Output:

```
Integer value: 10
Float value: 3.14
Char value: A
```

Explanation of Output:

- **First**: The union `data1` is assigned the integer value `10`, so when we print `data1.intVal`, it outputs `10`.
- **Second**: The union's `floatVal` member is assigned the value `3.14`. This overwrites the previous value of `intVal`, and when we print `data1.floatVal`, it outputs `3.14`.
- **Third**: The union's `charVal` member is assigned the character `'A'`. This overwrites the previous value of `floatVal`, and when we print `data1.charVal`, it outputs `'A'`.

Since all members of a union share the same memory space, only the last assigned member holds a valid value. The previous values are overwritten as new values are assigned to the union.

Key Points:

- **Memory Sharing**: All members of a union share the same memory space. The size of the union is the size of its largest member.
- **Overwriting Behavior**: When a new value is assigned to a union member, it overwrites the previous value stored in the union.
- **Accessing Members**: Only the last assigned member contains the valid data. The other members hold undefined values.

This makes unions useful when we need to store different types of data, but only one of them will be used at any given time.

Array of Structures

An **array of structures** is a collection of multiple instances of a structure. You can use an array to store several objects of the same structure type. This is particularly useful when you need to work with a collection of related data.

Syntax for Array of Structures:
```
struct structure_name {
    data_type member1;
    data_type member2;
    // more members...
};

structure_name array_name[size];
```

Example of Array of Structures:
```
#include <iostream>
using namespace std;

struct Student {
    int id;
```

```
        string name;
};

int main() {
    // Array of structures
    Student students[3] = {
        {101, "Alice"},
        {102, "Bob"},
        {103, "Charlie"}
    };

    // Accessing elements in the array of structures
    for (int i = 0; i < 3; i++) {
        cout << "Student ID: " << students[i].id << ", Name: " <<
students[i].name << endl;
    }

    return 0;
}
```
Output:
```
Student ID: 101, Name: Alice
Student ID: 102, Name: Bob
Student ID: 103, Name: Charlie
```

In this example:

- students is an array of Student structures.
- Each element in the array stores a Student object, and we access its members using
  students[i].id and students[i].name.

2. Nested Structures

A **nested structure** is when one structure contains another structure as a member. This helps in modeling more complex data types.

Syntax for Nested Structures:
```
struct Address {
    string street;
    string city;
    int pinCode;
};

struct Student {
    int id;
    string name;
    Address address;   // Nested structure
};
```

```cpp
#include <iostream>
using namespace std;

struct Address {
    string street;
    string city;
    int pinCode;
};

struct Student {
    int id;
    string name;
    Address address;   // Nested structure
};

int main() {
    // Initializing a structure with a nested structure
    Student student1 = {101, "John", {"Main St", "New York", 12345}};

    // Accessing nested structure elements
    cout << "Student Name: " << student1.name << endl;
    cout << "Street: " << student1.address.street << endl;
    cout << "City: " << student1.address.city << endl;
    cout << "Pin Code: " << student1.address.pinCode << endl;

    return 0;
}
```
Output:
```
Student Name: John
Street: Main St
City: New York
Pin Code: 12345
```

In this example:

- Student **structure contains a nested structure** Address.
- **We can access nested members using** student1.address.street,
  student1.address.city, **etc.**

---

3. Passing and Returning Structures from Functions

1. Passing Structures to Functions:

You can pass structures to functions **by value** or **by reference**:

- **By Value**: A copy of the structure is passed to the function.
- **By Reference**: A reference to the original structure is passed, which is more efficient.

```
#include <iostream>
using namespace std;

struct Student {
    int id;
    string name;
};

void display(Student s) {
    cout << "Student ID: " << s.id << ", Name: " << s.name << endl;
}

int main() {
    Student student1 = {101, "Alice"};
    display(student1); // Passing by value

    return 0;
}
```

Output:
```
Student ID: 101, Name: Alice
```

In this case, a copy of `student1` is passed to the `display` function.

Example of Passing Structure by Reference:
```
#include <iostream>
using namespace std;

struct Student {
    int id;
    string name;
};

void update(Student &s) {
    s.id = 102;  // Modifying original structure
    s.name = "Bob";
}

int main() {
    Student student1 = {101, "Alice"};
    update(student1); // Passing by reference

    cout << "Updated Student ID: " << student1.id << ", Name: " <<
student1.name << endl;

    return 0;
}
```

Output:
```
Updated Student ID: 102, Name: Bob
```

In this example:

- student1 is passed by reference, so any changes made in the update function are reflected in the original student1 structure.

---

2. Returning Structures from Functions:

You can also **return a structure** from a function. The function will return a structure, which can be assigned to a structure variable.

Example of Returning a Structure from a Function:

```cpp
#include <iostream>
using namespace std;

struct Student {
    int id;
    string name;
};

Student getStudent() {
    Student s = {103, "Charlie"};
    return s; // Returning structure
}

int main() {
    Student student1 = getStudent();
    cout << "Student ID: " << student1.id << ", Name: " << student1.name
<< endl;

    return 0;
}
```
Output:
```
Student ID: 103, Name: Charlie
```

In this example:

- The function getStudent returns a Student structure.
- The returned structure is assigned to student1 in the main function.

Summary:

- **Array of Structures** allows you to store multiple structures in an array and access their members.
- **Nested Structures** help in organizing more complex data by allowing one structure to contain another.
- **Passing Structures** to functions can be done either by value (copy) or by reference (efficient).
- **Returning Structures** from functions allows you to return a complex data type from a function.

Structure and Union Combinations

In C++, you can combine **structures** and **unions** to create more complex data types. This allows you to benefit from both data structures' properties. A **structure** provides different data members with individual memory locations, while a **union** shares memory between its members, meaning only one member can hold a value at a time.

Example of Structure and Union Combination:

In this example, we define a **union** that can store either an `int` or a `float`, and we use it inside a **structure**. The structure also has an `itemId` to uniquely identify each item.

```
#include <iostream>
using namespace std;

union Data {
    int intVal;
    float floatVal;
};

struct Item {
    int itemId;
    Data itemData; // Union inside a structure
};

int main() {
    Item item1;
    item1.itemId = 101;
    item1.itemData.intVal = 10; // Assigning value to union

    cout << "Item ID: " << item1.itemId << endl;
    cout << "Item Data (Int): " << item1.itemData.intVal << endl;

    item1.itemData.floatVal = 3.14; // Assigning new value to union
    cout << "Item Data (Float): " << item1.itemData.floatVal << endl;

    return 0;
}
```

Output:
```
Item ID: 101
Item Data (Int): 10
Item Data (Float): 3.14
```

In this example:

- The structure `Item` contains two members: `itemId` (an integer) and `itemData` (a union).
- The union `Data` can hold either an `int` or a `float`, but only one of them at a time.
- The `itemData` union is updated twice: first with an integer value, then with a floating-point value.
- The memory for `itemData` is shared between the `int` and `float`, meaning that assigning a new value to one overwrites the previous one.

---

25 MCQ ON THESE TOPICS

1. Understanding Structures and Unions

1. What is a structure in C/C++?
   a) A collection of related variables of the same type
   b) A collection of related variables of different types
   c) A method to define constants
   d) A predefined library function
   Answer: b
2. Which keyword is used to define a structure in C/C++?
   a) struct
   b) structure
   c) union
   d) class
   Answer: a
3. What is a union in C/C++?
   a) A collection of variables of different types sharing the same memory location
   b) A collection of variables of the same type
   c) A predefined structure type
   d) A dynamic data type
   Answer: a
4. How is memory allocated in a union?
   a) Based on the largest data member
   b) Based on the smallest data member
   c) Equal memory for all members
   d) Dynamically allocated
   Answer: a

5. Which of the following is a key difference between a structure and a union?
   a) Structures allocate separate memory for each member, unions share memory among members.
   b) Structures are faster than unions.
   c) Unions do not support functions.
   d) Structures cannot be nested.
   Answer: a

2. Declaring, Initializing, and Using Structures and Unions

6. How do you declare a structure in C++?
   a) `struct structName {};`
   b) `structure structName {};`
   c) `union structName {};`
   d) `class structName {};`
   Answer: a

7. How do you access a member of a structure?
   a) Using the `.` operator
   b) Using the `->` operator
   c) Using the `&` operator
   d) Using the `*` operator
   Answer: a

8. Can a structure be initialized at the time of declaration?
   a) Yes, by using an initializer list
   b) No, structures cannot be initialized
   c) Only in C++ but not in C
   d) Only using pointers
   Answer: a

9. What is the correct way to initialize a union?
   a) `unionName u = {value};`
   b) `union unionName(value);`
   c) `u = {value};`
   d) `u(value);`
   Answer: a

10. Which of the following is valid syntax for declaring a union?
    a) `union unionName { int a; float b; };`
    b) `union { int a, b; };`
    c) `unionName { int a; float b; };`
    d) `union unionName(int a, float b);`
    Answer: a

3. Array of Structures and Nested Structures

11. What is an array of structures?
    a) A collection of structures of the same type
    b) A structure containing an array
    c) A structure containing multiple data types
    d) An array with multiple data types
    Answer: a

12. How do you access the members of a structure within an array of structures?
    a) `arrayName[index].memberName`
    b) `arrayName->memberName`
    c) `arrayName[index]->memberName`
    d) `arrayName.memberName[index]`
    Answer: a

13. Which of the following correctly declares an array of structures?
    a) `structName arr[5];`
    b) `array[5] structName;`
    c) `struct structName array[5];`
    d) `array structName[5];`
    Answer: a

14. What is a nested structure?
    a) A structure containing another structure as a member
    b) A structure with dynamic memory allocation
    c) A structure defined inside a function
    d) A structure with variable-sized members
    Answer: a

15. How can you access a member of a nested structure?
    a) `struct1.struct2.memberName`
    b) `struct1->struct2.memberName`
    c) `struct1.struct2->memberName`
    d) `struct1.memberName.struct2`
    Answer: a

4. Passing and Returning Structures from Functions

16. Can a structure be passed to a function?
    a) Yes, either by value or by reference
    b) No, structures cannot be passed to functions
    c) Only by value
    d) Only by reference
    Answer: a

17. What happens when a structure is passed by value?
    a) A copy of the structure is passed to the function.
    b) The original structure is modified.

c) The function receives the address of the structure.
d) The structure is passed as a constant.
Answer: a

18. How can a structure be returned from a function?
    a) By defining the function return type as the structure type
    b) By returning a pointer to the structure
    c) By using a void return type
    d) Both a and b
    Answer: d

19. Which of the following functions returns a structure?
    a) `structName func();`
    b) `struct funcName();`
    c) `structName* func();`
    d) `struct structName* func();`
    Answer: a

20. Can a structure contain a pointer to itself?
    a) Yes
    b) No
    c) Only in C++
    d) Only in dynamically allocated structures
    Answer: a

5. Structure and Union Combinations

21. Can a union be a member of a structure?
    a) Yes
    b) No
    c) Only if defined globally
    d) Only in C++
    Answer: a

22. Can a structure be a member of a union?
    a) Yes
    b) No
    c) Only if the structure is global
    d) Only if it has static members
    Answer: a

23. What happens when a union contains a structure?
    a) The size of the union is determined by the size of the structure if it is the largest member.
    b) The structure members are individually allocated memory.
    c) The structure cannot be accessed.
    d) The union size becomes zero.
    Answer: a

24. Which of the following is a valid combination of structure and union?
    a) A structure containing a union as a member
    b) A union containing a structure as a member
    c) Both a and b
    d) None of the above
    Answer: c
25. What is the primary purpose of using a combination of structures and unions?
    a) To save memory by sharing and organizing data efficiently
    b) To enable dynamic memory allocation
    c) To increase computation speed
    d) To define recursive data types
    Answer: a

CHAPTER-6

POINTERS AND REFERENCES IN C++

In C++, pointers and references are key concepts that offer powerful memory management capabilities, enable pass-by-reference for functions, and facilitate dynamic memory operations. Here's an overview of each concept with examples.

Pointer Variables and Simple Pointer Operations

A **pointer** is a variable that holds the memory address of another variable. By using pointers, you can directly access and modify the values stored in the computer's memory.

Pointer Declaration:
```
type *pointer_name;
```

This declares a pointer variable that can store the address of a variable of the specified type.

Example of Pointer Initialization and Operations:
```cpp
#include <iostream>
using namespace std;

int main() {
    int num = 10;
    int *ptr = &num;  // Pointer ptr stores the address of num

    cout << "Value of num: " << num << endl;
    cout << "Address of num: " << &num << endl;
    cout << "Value at the address of ptr: " << *ptr << endl;  //
Dereferencing ptr to get value of num

    return 0;
}
```
Output:
```
Value of num: 10
Address of num: 0x7fffc27d69ac   (memory address)
Value at the address of ptr: 10
```

Explanation:

- **&num**: This represents the **address of** the variable num.
- **ptr**: The pointer stores the **address of** the variable num.
- ***ptr**: This is **dereferencing** the pointer, which means accessing the value stored at the memory address that ptr holds. In this case, it accesses the value of num.

Key Concepts in Pointer Operations:

1. **Dereferencing (*ptr)**: Accessing the value at the address the pointer points to.
2. **Address-of (&)**: Getting the memory address of a variable.
3. **Pointer Initialization**: Pointers are initialized with the address of a variable using the **&** operator.

Pointers are very efficient for tasks such as dynamic memory allocation, handling large arrays, and passing data to functions without copying the values.

Pointers to Pointers and Pointers to Structures in C++

Pointers to pointers and pointers to structures are important concepts that help in advanced memory management and handling data structures efficiently. Let's explore these concepts in more detail with examples.

Pointers to Pointers

A **pointer to a pointer** is a pointer that stores the address of another pointer. It is commonly used when you need to modify the pointer itself or when dealing with multi-level data structures. Essentially, a pointer to a pointer allows indirect access to the data.

Example of Pointer to Pointer:

```cpp
#include <iostream>
using namespace std;

int main() {
    int num = 5;
    int *ptr = &num;        // Pointer to integer
    int **ptr2 = &ptr;      // Pointer to pointer

    cout << "Value of num: " << num << endl;
    cout << "Value using ptr: " << *ptr << endl;
    cout << "Value using ptr2: " << **ptr2 << endl;   // Dereferencing
twice

    return 0;
}
```

Output:
```
Value of num: 5
Value using ptr: 5
Value using ptr2: 5
```

Explanation:

- **ptr**: This pointer stores the **address of num**, and you can access the value of num by dereferencing ptr using *ptr.
- **ptr2**: This is a pointer to a pointer. It stores the **address of the pointer ptr**. To access the value of num via ptr2, you need to dereference it twice: first to access ptr and second to access the value num (i.e., **ptr2).

Key Concepts:

- **Dereferencing a pointer to pointer (**ptr2)**: This accesses the value stored at the address of the address that ptr2 points to (i.e., num).
- **Why use a pointer to pointer?**: This is useful when you want to modify the original pointer in a function or when working with dynamic memory allocation, like in 2D arrays or linked lists.

Pointers to Structures

A **pointer to a structure** is a pointer that holds the address of a structure variable. Using a pointer to a structure, you can access the structure's members using the **arrow operator (->).** This operator is used to access members of a structure when you have a pointer to that structure.

Example of Pointer to Structure:
```cpp
#include <iostream>
using namespace std;

struct Student {
    int id;
    string name;
};

int main() {
    Student student1 = {101, "Alice"};
    Student *ptr = &student1;  // Pointer to structure

    cout << "Student ID: " << ptr->id << endl;
    cout << "Student Name: " << ptr->name << endl;  // Accessing members
via pointer

    return 0;
}
```
Output:
```
Student ID: 101
Student Name: Alice
```

Explanation:

- **ptr**: This pointer holds the **address of the structure student1**.
- The **arrow operator (->)** is used to access the members of the structure through the pointer. In this case:
  - **ptr->id**: Accesses the id member of the structure student1.
  - **ptr->name**: Accesses the name member of the structure student1.

Key Concepts:

- **Arrow operator (->)**: This operator allows you to access the members of a structure when using a pointer to the structure. It is equivalent to dereferencing the pointer first and then accessing the member (i.e., (*ptr).id), but ptr->id is more convenient and commonly used.
- **Why use pointers to structures?**: Pointers to structures are used when you need to pass large structures to functions efficiently or when dealing with dynamic memory allocation (e.g., in linked lists, trees, etc.).

Both pointers to pointers and pointers to structures are powerful features in C++ that allow more flexible and efficient management of memory and data structures. Let me know if you would like more examples or explanations of specific scenarios!

Passing and Returning Pointers as Function Arguments in C++

In C++, **passing pointers** and **returning pointers** are essential concepts that enable direct memory manipulation, efficient data management, and dynamic memory handling. These techniques are especially useful for modifying data inside functions and working with dynamically allocated memory.

Passing Pointers to Functions

Passing a **pointer** to a function allows that function to directly access and modify the value of a variable stored in memory. This is different from passing variables by value, where the function only works with a copy of the data.

Example of Passing Pointer to a Function:
```
#include <iostream>
using namespace std;

void modifyValue(int *ptr) {
```

```
    *ptr = 20;   // Modifying the value of the variable at the pointer's
address
}

int main() {
    int num = 10;
    cout << "Before function call: " << num << endl;

    modifyValue(&num);   // Passing address of num to function

    cout << "After function call: " << num << endl;   // Modified value of
num

    return 0;
}
```
Output:
```
Before function call: 10
After function call: 20
```

Explanation:

- **&num**: The address of num is passed to the function modifyValue. This allows the function to access the actual memory location of num.
- **Inside modifyValue**: The function takes an integer pointer ptr. By dereferencing the pointer (*ptr), the value of num can be modified directly.
- **Effect**: The value of num is changed to 20 inside the function, and this change is reflected in the main function because the original memory address was passed.

Key Concept:

- **Passing by Reference via Pointer**: When you pass a pointer, you're passing the memory address of a variable, which allows the function to modify the original variable's value rather than working on a copy.

Returning Pointers from Functions

A function can return a **pointer**, which is particularly useful when dealing with **dynamically allocated memory** (memory allocated at runtime). When you return a pointer, the caller can use it to access the dynamically allocated memory.

Example of Returning a Pointer from a Function:
```
#include <iostream>
using namespace std;

int* getPointer() {
    int *ptr = new int(30);   // Dynamically allocating memory for an
integer
    return ptr;   // Returning the pointer }
```

```
int main() {
    int *ptr = getPointer();
    cout << "Value from returned pointer: " << *ptr << endl;

    delete ptr;   // Deallocating memory
    return 0;
}
```
Output:
```
Value from returned pointer: 30
```

Explanation:

- **new**: The `new` operator is used to dynamically allocate memory on the **heap** for an integer and initialize it with the value 30. The address of this allocated memory is stored in the pointer `ptr`.
- **Returning the Pointer**: The function `getPointer` returns the pointer `ptr` that holds the address of the dynamically allocated memory.
- **Dereferencing**: In `main()`, the pointer returned by `getPointer` is dereferenced using `*ptr` to access the value stored at that memory location (30).
- **delete**: After using the dynamically allocated memory, `delete ptr` is called to free the memory and avoid **memory leaks**.

Key Concepts:

- **Dynamic Memory Allocation**: The `new` operator is used to allocate memory dynamically at runtime. This allows you to allocate memory based on the needs of your program rather than at compile time.
- **Memory Deallocation**: The `delete` operator is used to free the dynamically allocated memory after it is no longer needed. Failing to do so results in memory leaks, where memory is wasted and unavailable for reuse.

Important Points to Remember:

- **Pass-by-Reference via Pointer**: Passing pointers allows direct modification of the original variable. It's efficient for large data structures or arrays.
- **Dynamic Memory**: Returning pointers is common when working with **dynamic memory** to ensure that the memory persists outside the scope of the function.
- **Memory Management**: Always remember to `delete` memory allocated with `new` to prevent memory leaks.

By using pointers in function arguments and return values, you can optimize memory usage and increase the flexibility of your C++ programs.

Using Arrays as Pointers in C++

In C++, an **array name** is essentially a pointer to its **first element**. This powerful feature allows arrays to be manipulated through pointer arithmetic. When you work with arrays and pointers together, you can access array elements efficiently without using array indices. Instead, pointer arithmetic can be applied.

Array as Pointer

An array in C++ is closely tied to pointers. Specifically:

- The name of an array (e.g., `arr`) represents a **pointer to its first element**.
- You can use this pointer to access and manipulate the array elements through **pointer arithmetic**.

For example:

- **arr** is treated as the address of `arr[0]`.
- **&arr[0]** is equivalent to `arr`.

When you use a pointer, you can access array elements by performing arithmetic on the pointer value.

Example of Using Arrays as Pointers

```cpp
#include <iostream>
using namespace std;

int main() {
    int arr[] = {1, 2, 3, 4, 5};
    int *ptr = arr;   // Pointer to the first element of the array

    for (int i = 0; i < 5; i++) {
        cout << "Element at index " << i << ": " << *(ptr + i) << endl;
// Pointer arithmetic
    }

    return 0;
}
```
Output:
```
Element at index 0: 1
Element at index 1: 2
Element at index 2: 3
Element at index 3: 4
Element at index 4: 5
```

Explanation:

- **`ptr = arr`**: Here, `ptr` is initialized to point to the first element of the array `arr[0]`. This is equivalent to writing `ptr = &arr[0]`. So, `ptr` holds the memory address of the first element of the array.
- **Pointer Arithmetic**: In the `for` loop, the expression `*(ptr + i)` is used to access each array element:
    - `ptr + i`: Moves the pointer `i` positions ahead. This essentially "shifts" the pointer to point to the `i`-th element of the array.
    - `*(ptr + i)`: Dereferences the pointer, accessing the value at that memory address.
- **Result**: This code effectively prints each element of the array by using pointer arithmetic instead of array indexing.

Key Concepts:

1. **Pointer to the First Element**: The name of the array (`arr`) is a pointer to the first element. This is why `arr` and `&arr[0]` are equivalent in most cases.
2. **Pointer Arithmetic**: You can perform arithmetic operations on pointers to access different elements in an array. The pointer will "move" by the size of the type it points to (e.g., moving from one `int` to the next `int`).
3. **Dereferencing**: `*(ptr + i)` dereferences the pointer at the `i`-th element, returning the value stored there. This allows accessing array elements without using the array index `arr[i]`.

Important Notes:

- **Array Indexing vs. Pointer Arithmetic**: While both `arr[i]` and `*(arr + i)` do the same thing (access the `i`-th element), using pointers gives you more flexibility, especially in situations involving dynamic memory or complex data structures.
- **Pointer to Array**: A pointer to an array (or to the first element) provides a mechanism to loop through or manipulate the array dynamically.

Using pointers with arrays in this way is highly efficient and allows for more advanced data manipulation and memory control in C++.

Understanding References and their Use in Functions

In C++, **references** provide a mechanism for passing arguments to functions in a way that avoids the need to return a value or use pointers. A reference is essentially an **alias** for another variable, meaning it doesn't create a new variable but rather acts as a second name for an existing variable. This can help modify the original variable directly and is especially useful for performance reasons when working with large data types.

Reference Declaration

A reference is declared using the `&` symbol. It binds directly to an existing variable, and any changes made to the reference affect the original variable.

```
type &reference_name = variable;
```

For example:

```
int num = 10;
int &ref = num;   // 'ref' is now a reference to 'num'
```

In this example, `ref` is a reference to `num`, meaning that modifying `ref` will directly modify `num`.

Passing by Reference

When you pass a variable to a function by reference, the function does not receive a copy of the variable. Instead, it works directly with the original variable, which means any changes made to the parameter inside the function will be reflected in the original variable outside the function.

This is different from **pass-by-value**, where a copy of the variable is passed, and any changes made inside the function do not affect the original variable.

Example of Passing by Reference
```
#include <iostream>
using namespace std;

void modifyValue(int &ref) {
    ref = 20;   // Modifies the original variable
}

int main() {
    int num = 10;
    cout << "Before function call: " << num << endl;
```

```
    modifyValue(num);   // Passing by reference

    cout << "After function call: " << num << endl;   // Modified value of
num

    return 0;
}
```
Output:
```
Before function call: 10
After function call: 20
```

Explanation:

- **int &ref**: Here, `ref` is a reference to the variable `num`. The `&` in the function signature indicates that `ref` is a reference to `num`.
- **modifyValue(num)**: When `num` is passed to the function `modifyValue`, the function receives a reference to `num`. This means any modification to `ref` will modify `num` as well.
- **Inside the function**, `ref = 20;` changes the value of `num` to `20` directly because `ref` is just another name for `num`.
- **After the function call**, the value of `num` is updated to `20`, and it reflects the changes made within the function. This is the key difference between **pass-by-value** and **pass-by-reference**.

Key Points about References:

1. **Alias for a Variable**: A reference acts as an alias for another variable. It refers directly to the original variable and does not create a copy.
2. **Modifying the Original Variable**: Changes to the reference affect the original variable. This is useful in situations where you want a function to modify an argument's value or work with large objects without copying them.
3. **No Null References**: Unlike pointers, references cannot be `null`. A reference must always refer to an object, and once it is bound to a variable, it cannot be changed to refer to another variable.
4. **Performance Benefit**: Passing large data structures (like large arrays or classes) by reference rather than by value can improve performance by avoiding unnecessary copying of data.

---

1. Pointer Variables and Simple Pointer Operations

1. What is a pointer in C++?
   a) A variable that stores the address of another variable
   b) A variable that stores the value of another variable
   c) A function that operates on addresses
   d) A keyword in C++
   Answer: a
2. Which operator is used to get the address of a variable?
   a) *
   b) &
   c) ->
   d) []
   Answer: b
3. Which operator is used to access the value at the address stored in a pointer?
   a) *
   b) &
   c) ->
   d) []
   Answer: a
4. What is the default value of an uninitialized pointer in C++?
   a) NULL
   b) 0
   c) Garbage value
   d) Undefined
   Answer: c
5. How do you declare a pointer to an integer?
   a) `int *p;`
   b) `int p;`
   c) `pointer<int> p;`
   d) `int &p;`
   Answer: a

2. Pointers to Pointers and Pointers to Structures

6. What is a pointer to a pointer?
   a) A pointer storing the address of another pointer
   b) A pointer storing the value of another pointer
   c) A pointer storing the size of another pointer
   d) None of the above
   Answer: a

7. How do you declare a pointer to a pointer in C++?
   a) `int **ptr;`
   b) `int *ptr*;`
   c) `pointer<int*> ptr;`
   d) `int ptr**;`
   Answer: a
8. Which of the following is the correct way to access a structure member using a pointer?
   a) `ptr->memberName`
   b) `*ptr.memberName`
   c) `ptr.memberName`
   d) `ptr->*memberName`
   Answer: a
9. What is the output of the following code?

```
int x = 10;
int *p = &x;
int **q = &p;
cout << **q;
```

   a) 10
   b) Address of x
   c) Address of p
   d) Compilation error
   Answer: a

10. Can you assign the address of a structure to a pointer?
    a) Yes
    b) No
    c) Only in C++
    d) Only in C
    Answer: a

3. Passing and Returning Pointers as Function Arguments

11. Can you pass a pointer as an argument to a function?
    a) Yes, by value or by reference
    b) No
    c) Only by reference
    d) Only in C++
    Answer: a
12. What happens when you pass a pointer to a function by value?
    a) A copy of the pointer is passed to the function
    b) The original pointer is passed to the function
    c) The pointer becomes NULL

d) The function can't modify the pointer

Answer: a

13. How can a pointer be returned from a function?
    a) By defining the return type as a pointer type
    b) By using the `void` return type
    c) By returning a reference to the pointer
    d) Both a and c

Answer: a

14. Which of the following is a valid function declaration for passing a pointer?
    a) `void func(int *ptr);`
    b) `void func(int &ptr);`
    c) `void func(int ptr*);`
    d) `void func(int ptr&);`

Answer: a

15. What is the primary advantage of passing pointers to functions?
    a) Saves memory by not copying large data structures
    b) Prevents the function from modifying the data
    c) Simplifies syntax
    d) Avoids dynamic memory allocation

Answer: a

4. Using Arrays as Pointers

16. How can you treat an array as a pointer?
    a) By using the array name as a pointer
    b) By declaring a pointer and assigning the array name to it
    c) Both a and b
    d) Arrays cannot be treated as pointers

Answer: c

17. Which of the following correctly accesses the third element of an array using pointers?
    a) `*(arr + 2)`
    b) `*arr[2]`
    c) `arr[2*]`
    d) `arr*(2)`

Answer: a

18. What is the output of the following code?

```
int arr[] = {1, 2, 3};
int *p = arr;
cout << *(p + 1);
```

    a) 1
    b) 2
    c) 3

d) Compilation error
Answer: b

19. Which of the following statements is true about arrays and pointers?
    a) The array name is a pointer to the first element of the array.
    b) Arrays cannot be accessed using pointers.
    c) Pointers and arrays are completely unrelated.
    d) An array name is a constant pointer to the last element of the array.
    Answer: a
20. How do you increment a pointer to move to the next element in an array?
    a) `ptr++`
    b) `ptr+1`
    c) `ptr += sizeof(dataType)`
    d) All of the above
    Answer: a

5. Understanding References and their Use in Functions

21. What is a reference in C++?
    a) An alias for an already existing variable
    b) A pointer to a variable
    c) A dynamic memory allocation mechanism
    d) A keyword for memory access
    Answer: a
22. Which symbol is used to declare a reference?
    a) &
    b) *
    c) ->
    d) ::
    Answer: a
23. Can a reference be NULL in C++?
    a) No
    b) Yes
    c) Only in dynamically allocated memory
    d) Only if it's a constant reference
    Answer: a
24. What is the primary difference between pointers and references?
    a) References cannot be reassigned, pointers can.
    b) References use memory, pointers do not.
    c) Pointers are faster than references.
    d) References can point to NULL, pointers cannot.
    Answer: a

25. How are references useful in functions?
    a) They allow passing large data structures without copying them.
    b) They allow modification of original variables directly.
    c) They make the syntax cleaner.
    d) All of the above
    Answer: d

CHAPTER-7

MEMORY ALLOCATION IN C++

Memory management in C++ is a crucial part of programming, and it can be done in two main ways: **Static Memory Allocation** and **Dynamic Memory Allocation**. Let's explore both types in detail and understand their differences, along with how memory is managed using functions like `malloc`, `calloc`, `free`, `new`, and `delete`.

---

1. Static Memory Allocation:

- **Definition**: Static memory allocation occurs at **compile-time**. This means the size of memory must be known before the program runs and cannot be changed while the program is executing.
- **Characteristics**:
    - Memory is allocated for variables or arrays during the program's compilation.
    - The size and type of memory to be allocated must be defined ahead of time.
    - Memory is automatically managed (i.e., it is released when the variable goes out of scope).
    - This type of memory allocation is fast but lacks flexibility.
- **Use Cases**:
    - Global variables, local variables in functions, and arrays with fixed sizes.
    - Suitable when the size of data structures is fixed or known in advance.

Example:
```cpp
#include <iostream>
using namespace std;

int num = 10;   // Static memory allocation (global variable)
int arr[5];     // Static array allocation (fixed size at compile time)

int main() {
    cout << "Global num: " << num << endl;
    for (int i = 0; i < 5; i++) {
        arr[i] = i + 1;  // Initializing static array
    }

    // Print array elements
    for (int i = 0; i < 5; i++) {
        cout << "Element " << i << ": " << arr[i] << endl;
    }

    return 0;
}
```

Explanation:

- `num` is statically allocated with a fixed size of 10.
- `arr` is a static array of size 5, which is allocated at compile-time.
- You cannot change the size of `arr` at runtime since it is fixed.

---

2. Dynamic Memory Allocation:

- **Definition**: Dynamic memory allocation occurs during **runtime** (while the program is executing). This allows for flexibility as memory can be allocated or deallocated as needed during the program's execution.
- **Characteristics**:
    - Memory is allocated when the program is running, which provides flexibility to use memory efficiently.
    - The size of the memory can be determined during execution, making it ideal for scenarios where the size is unknown at compile-time.
    - The programmer must explicitly allocate and deallocate memory, as failure to do so may lead to memory leaks or segmentation faults.
- **Use Cases**:
    - Suitable for cases where the size of data structures, such as arrays or linked lists, may vary during execution.
    - Used when you need to allocate large memory blocks dynamically, especially for arrays or objects that could change in size.

Example:
```cpp
#include <iostream>
using namespace std;

int main() {
    int* ptr = new int;   // Allocating memory dynamically for one integer
    *ptr = 100;            // Assigning value to dynamically allocated
memory

    int* arr = new int[5];   // Allocating memory dynamically for an array
of 5 integers
    for (int i = 0; i < 5; i++) {
        arr[i] = i * 10;     // Assign values to the dynamically allocated
array
    }

    cout << "Dynamically allocated integer: " << *ptr << endl;
    for (int i = 0; i < 5; i++) {
        cout << "Dynamically allocated array element " << i << ": " <<
arr[i] << endl;
    }

    delete ptr;   // Deallocating memory for the single integer
    delete[] arr;   // Deallocating memory for the array
```

```
    return 0;
}
```

Explanation:

- `ptr` is a pointer to a dynamically allocated integer. The `new` operator is used to allocate memory at runtime for the integer, and the value is assigned.
- `arr` is a pointer to a dynamically allocated array of integers. The size of the array (5 elements) is determined at runtime, and values are assigned dynamically.
- After the memory is used, it is deallocated using the `delete` operator for single variables and `delete[]` for arrays to avoid memory leaks.

Key Differences Between Static and Dynamic Memory Allocation:

Feature	Static Memory Allocation	Dynamic Memory Allocation
Time of Allocation	Allocated at compile-time.	Allocated at runtime.
Size	Fixed at compile-time and cannot be changed.	Can be changed during execution.
Flexibility	Less flexible, as memory size must be predefined.	More flexible, allows allocation and deallocation as needed.
Management	Automatically managed by the compiler (released when scope ends).	Must be manually managed using `new` and `delete`.
Example	Global variables, local variables, static arrays.	Arrays, dynamic data structures like linked lists.
Performance	Faster, but inflexible.	Slight overhead due to runtime allocation and deallocation.

Using `malloc`, `calloc`, and `free` in C++

In C++ (and C), dynamic memory allocation is done using functions such as `malloc`, `calloc`, and `free`, which are part of the C standard library (`cstdlib`). These functions are used for allocating and deallocating memory on the heap. Let's go over each function in detail.

1. `malloc()` (Memory Allocation):

- **Definition**: `malloc` stands for "memory allocation". It is used to allocate a block of memory of a specified size. However, the allocated memory is **not initialized**, meaning it could contain garbage values.
- **Syntax**:

```
void* malloc(size_t size);
```

-    o `size`: The size in bytes of the memory block to be allocated.
- **Return Value**: It returns a pointer to the allocated memory block. If the allocation fails, it returns `NULL`.

Example:
```cpp
#include <iostream>
#include <cstdlib>  // For malloc
using namespace std;

int main() {
    int* ptr = (int*)malloc(sizeof(int));  // Allocating memory for one integer
    if (ptr == NULL) {
        cout << "Memory allocation failed!" << endl;
    } else {
        *ptr = 100;  // Assigning a value to the allocated memory
        cout << "Allocated value: " << *ptr << endl;
    }

    free(ptr);  // Deallocating memory
    return 0;
}
```

Explanation:

- `malloc(sizeof(int))`: Allocates memory for a single integer.
- The memory is not initialized, so the value stored in `ptr` may be unpredictable if not assigned explicitly.
- Always check if the allocation succeeded by verifying if the pointer is `NULL`.
- The memory is freed using `free(ptr)` once it's no longer needed.

---

2. `calloc()` (Contiguous Allocation):

- **Definition**: `calloc` stands for "contiguous allocation". It is used to allocate a block of memory for an array of elements. Unlike `malloc`, `calloc` **initializes all elements to zero**.

- **Syntax**:

```
void* calloc(size_t num_elements, size_t size_of_element);
```

  - o num_elements: The number of elements to allocate.
  - o size_of_element: The size of each element in bytes.
- **Return Value**: It returns a pointer to the allocated memory block. If the allocation fails, it returns NULL.

Example:
```cpp
#include <iostream>
#include <cstdlib>  // For calloc
using namespace std;

int main() {
    int* arr = (int*)calloc(5, sizeof(int));  // Allocating memory for 5
integers, initialized to 0
    if (arr == NULL) {
        cout << "Memory allocation failed!" << endl;
    } else {
        // Printing values of array elements (initialized to 0)
        for (int i = 0; i < 5; i++) {
            cout << "Element " << i << ": " << arr[i] << endl;
        }
    }

    free(arr);  // Deallocating memory
    return 0;
}
```

Explanation:

- calloc(5, sizeof(int)): Allocates memory for 5 integers, initializing each of them to zero.
- If the allocation is successful, it initializes the array elements to zero.
- Always check if the allocation was successful before using the memory.
- The memory is deallocated using free(arr) when done.

3. `free()` (Deallocating Memory):

- **Definition**: `free` is used to deallocate memory that was previously allocated by `malloc`, `calloc`, or `realloc`. It releases the memory back to the heap, making it available for future allocations.
- **Syntax**:

```
void free(void* ptr);
```

  - `ptr`: A pointer to the memory block to be freed.
- **Important Notes**:
  - You should only call `free` on memory that was allocated dynamically using `malloc`, `calloc`, or `realloc`.
  - Calling `free` on memory that was not dynamically allocated (such as a local or statically allocated variable) can lead to undefined behavior.
  - After calling `free`, the pointer is still pointing to the same memory location, but it is now **dangling**. It's a good practice to set the pointer to `NULL` after freeing it.

Example:
```cpp
#include <iostream>
#include <cstdlib>  // For free
using namespace std;

int main() {
    int* ptr = (int*)malloc(sizeof(int));  // Allocating memory for one
integer
    if (ptr == NULL) {
        cout << "Memory allocation failed!" << endl;
    } else {
        *ptr = 100;
        cout << "Value: " << *ptr << endl;
    }

    free(ptr);  // Deallocating memory
    ptr = NULL; // Avoid dangling pointer by setting it to NULL

    return 0;
}
```

Explanation:

- After using the dynamically allocated memory (`*ptr = 100`), we use `free(ptr)` to deallocate the memory.
- Setting `ptr = NULL` helps avoid any future dereferencing of a dangling pointer, which could cause undefined behavior.

Using `new` and `delete` Operators in C++

C++ introduced the `new` and `delete` operators for dynamic memory allocation, offering a type-safe, more convenient alternative to `malloc`, `calloc`, and `free`. These operators not only allocate and deallocate memory but also handle constructor and destructor calls when working with classes.

---

1. `new` Operator (Dynamic Memory Allocation)

- **Definition**: The `new` operator allocates memory dynamically from the heap for a single variable or an array of variables. It also calls the constructor of a class (if applicable) to initialize the object.
- **Syntax**:
    - For a single variable:

      ```
      pointer_type* new (type);
      ```

    - For an array of variables:

      ```
      pointer_type* new (size_t size);
      ```

- **Exception Handling**: If memory allocation fails, `new` throws a `std::bad_alloc` exception (by default), making error handling easier than `malloc`, which returns `NULL` in case of failure.

Example (Allocating Single Variable):
```cpp
#include <iostream>
using namespace std;

int main() {
    int* ptr = new int;  // Allocating memory for one integer
    *ptr = 10;  // Assigning value to the allocated memory

    cout << "Value: " << *ptr << endl;

    delete ptr;  // Deallocating memory for the single variable
    return 0;
}
```

Example (Allocating Array):
```cpp
#include <iostream>
using namespace std;

int main() {
    int* arr = new int[5];  // Allocating memory for an array of 5 integers
    for (int i = 0; i < 5; i++) {
        arr[i] = i + 1;  // Assigning values to the array
    }
```

```
    for (int i = 0; i < 5; i++) {
        cout << "Element " << i << ": " << arr[i] << endl;
    }

    delete[] arr;  // Deallocating memory for the array
    return 0;
}
```

Explanation:

- `new int` allocates memory for a single integer, and `*ptr = 10` stores the value in the allocated memory.
- `new int[5]` allocates memory for an array of 5 integers.
- **delete** is used to deallocate memory for a single variable (`delete ptr`) or an array (`delete[] arr`).

2. `delete` Operator (Memory Deallocation)

- **Definition**: The `delete` operator is used to deallocate memory that was allocated by `new`. It also calls the destructor of a class (if applicable) before releasing memory. For arrays, `delete[]` is used.
- **Syntax**:
  - For deallocating a single variable:

    ```
    delete pointer;
    ```

  - For deallocating an array of variables:

    ```
    delete[] pointer;
    ```

Example:
```
#include <iostream>
using namespace std;

int main() {
    int* ptr = new int;  // Allocating memory
    *ptr = 100;  // Assigning a value

    cout << "Value before delete: " << *ptr << endl;

    delete ptr;  // Deallocating memory
    return 0;
}
```

Explanation:

- `delete ptr` frees the memory allocated for the single integer.

- Always ensure that memory is deallocated using `delete` for single variables and `delete[]` for arrays to prevent memory leaks.

Comparison Between `malloc/calloc` and `new/delete`

Feature	malloc/calloc	new/delete
Memory Allocation	Allocates raw memory but does not call constructors.	Allocates memory and calls constructors for objects.
Initialization	`malloc` does not initialize memory, `calloc` does.	Memory is initialized only for objects, not primitive types.
Error Handling	Returns `NULL` on failure.	Throws `std::bad_alloc` exception on failure (default behavior).
Type Safety	Not type-safe (requires casting).	Type-safe (no casting required).
Memory Deallocation	`free()` function.	`delete` (for single variable), `delete[]` (for arrays).

25 MCQ ON THESE TOPICS

1. Static vs. Dynamic Memory Allocation

1. What is static memory allocation?
   a) Memory is allocated during program execution.
   b) Memory is allocated at compile-time.
   c) Memory is dynamically resized during execution.
   d) Memory is allocated using pointers.
   Answer: b
2. Which of the following is an example of static memory allocation?
   a) Using `malloc()`
   b) Using `new`
   c) Declaring variables with fixed sizes at compile-time
   d) Using `calloc()`
   Answer: c
3. Dynamic memory allocation is performed:
   a) At compile-time
   b) At runtime
   c) During linking

d) By the operating system before program execution
Answer: b

4. Which of the following requires manual memory management?
   a) Static memory allocation
   b) Dynamic memory allocation
   c) Both static and dynamic
   d) Neither static nor dynamic
   Answer: b

5. What is a key drawback of static memory allocation?
   a) It can only allocate memory for primitive data types.
   b) The size of memory must be predetermined.
   c) It is slower than dynamic memory allocation.
   d) It cannot be accessed using pointers.
   Answer: b

2. Using malloc, calloc, and free

6. What does `malloc()` do in C++?
   a) Allocates memory and initializes it to zero
   b) Allocates memory without initialization
   c) Frees allocated memory
   d) Allocates memory for static variables
   Answer: b

7. Which library is required for using `malloc()`, `calloc()`, and `free()` in C++?
   a) `<iostream>`
   b) `<cstdlib>`
   c) `<memory>`
   d) `<string>`
   Answer: b

8. What is the difference between `malloc()` and `calloc()`?
   a) `malloc()` allocates memory; `calloc()` frees memory.
   b) `calloc()` allocates zero-initialized memory; `malloc()` does not.
   c) `malloc()` allocates memory for arrays; `calloc()` does not.
   d) They are identical.
   Answer: b

9. Which function is used to free dynamically allocated memory?
   a) `release()`
   b) `deallocate()`
   c) `free()`
   d) `delete`
   Answer: c

10. What is the correct syntax for allocating memory for an integer array using `calloc()`?
    a) `int *arr = (int *)calloc(5);`

b) `int *arr = (int *)calloc(5, sizeof(int));`
c) `int arr = calloc(5, sizeof(int));`
d) `int arr[5] = calloc(5);`
Answer: b

11. What happens if you try to access memory that has been freed using `free()`?
    a) Undefined behavior
    b) Memory is reallocated automatically
    c) Compilation error
    d) Program terminates with a segmentation fault
    Answer: a

12. Which of the following is true about `malloc()`?
    a) It initializes memory to zero.
    b) It allocates memory but does not initialize it.
    c) It frees memory automatically after use.
    d) It allocates memory for static variables.
    Answer: b

13. Which of the following is true about `calloc()`?
    a) It allocates memory but does not initialize it.
    b) It initializes all allocated memory to zero.
    c) It cannot allocate memory for arrays.
    d) It requires `<iostream>` header file.
    Answer: b

3. Using new and delete Operators

14. What does the `new` operator do in C++?
    a) Allocates memory and returns the address of the allocated memory
    b) Allocates memory and initializes it to zero
    c) Allocates memory for static variables
    d) Frees dynamically allocated memory
    Answer: a

15. How do you free memory allocated with the `new` operator?
    a) Using `free()`
    b) Using `delete`
    c) Using `delete[]`
    d) Both b and c
    Answer: d

16. Which of the following is the correct syntax to allocate memory for an integer using `new`?
    a) `int *ptr = (int *)new;`
    b) `int ptr = new int;`
    c) `int *ptr = new int;`
    d) `int *ptr = new(int);`
    Answer: c

17. How do you allocate memory for an array of 10 integers using `new`?
    a) `int *arr = new int[10];`
    b) `int arr = new int(10);`
    c) `int *arr = new[10] int;`
    d) `int arr[10] = new int;`
    Answer: a
18. What happens if you forget to delete memory allocated with `new`?
    a) The program terminates immediately.
    b) The program crashes.
    c) Memory leaks occur.
    d) The memory is automatically freed.
    Answer: c
19. Which of the following is the correct way to delete an array allocated using `new`?
    a) `delete arr;`
    b) `delete arr[];`
    c) `delete[] arr;`
    d) `free(arr);`
    Answer: c
20. What is the output of the following code?

```
int *p = new int(5);
cout << *p;
delete p;
```

    a) 0
    b) 5
    c) Undefined
    d) Compilation error
    Answer: b

21. What is the difference between `malloc()` and `new`?
    a) `malloc()` initializes memory; `new` does not.
    b) `new` initializes memory; `malloc()` does not.
    c) `malloc()` requires `delete` to free memory; `new` requires `free()`.
    d) `malloc()` and `new` are identical.
    Answer: b
22. Which of the following statements is true about the `delete` operator?
    a) It can only delete scalar variables.
    b) It can delete both scalar and array variables.
    c) It cannot be used for arrays.
    d) It automatically deletes all pointers in a program.
    Answer: b
23. How does `new` differ from `malloc()` in terms of type safety?
    a) `new` is type-safe; `malloc()` is not.
    b) `malloc()` is type-safe; `new` is not.
    c) Both are type-safe.

d) Neither is type-safe.

Answer: a

24. What is the correct way to delete a pointer that points to a structure allocated using `new`?

a) `delete ptr;`

b) `delete *ptr;`

c) `delete &ptr;`

d) `free(ptr);`

Answer: a

25. Which of the following does not support dynamic memory allocation?

a) `new`

b) `malloc()`

c) `calloc()`

d) Static variables

Answer: d

CHAPTER-8

FILE I/O AND PREPROCESSOR DIRECTIVES IN C++

In C++, file handling and preprocessor directives are essential for managing file operations and controlling the compilation process, respectively. Here, we explore how to handle file input and output, random file access, and various preprocessor directives.

1. File Handling in C++

C++ provides file handling through the `<fstream>` library, which offers three primary classes for file operations:

- **`ifstream`**: Used for reading files (input file stream).
- **`ofstream`**: Used for writing to files (output file stream).
- **`fstream`**: Used for both reading and writing to files.

Opening a File

Before performing any operations on a file, you need to open it using the appropriate class. Here's an example of how to open a file for reading and writing:

```
#include <iostream>
#include <fstream>
using namespace std;

int main() {
    // Opening files
    ifstream inputFile("input.txt");  // Open file for reading
    ofstream outputFile("output.txt");  // Open file for writing

    // Check if files are opened successfully
    if (!inputFile) {
        cout << "Error opening input file!" << endl;
        return 1;  // Return an error code if file opening fails
    }

    if (!outputFile) {
        cout << "Error opening output file!" << endl;
        return 1;  // Handle file open failure
    }

    // File operations will go here

    // Close files after operations
    inputFile.close();
    outputFile.close();
```

```
    return 0;}
```
Reading and Writing Text Files

You can use `ifstream` to read from a file and `ofstream` to write to a file. Here's an example:

```cpp
#include <iostream>
#include <fstream>
using namespace std;

int main() {
    // Writing to a file
    ofstream outputFile("output.txt");
    if (outputFile.is_open()) {
        outputFile << "Hello, File I/O in C++!" << endl;
        outputFile.close();  // Close the file after writing
    }

    // Reading from a file
    ifstream inputFile("output.txt");
    string line;
    if (inputFile.is_open()) {
        while (getline(inputFile, line)) {
            cout << line << endl;  // Print each line read from the file
        }
        inputFile.close();  // Close the file after reading
    }

    return 0;
}
```
Random Access in Files

C++ allows random access to files using the `fstream` class. You can move the file pointer to a specific position within the file using `seekg()` (for reading) or `seekp()` (for writing). You can also use `tellg()` and `tellp()` to check the current position of the file pointer.

```cpp
#include <iostream>
#include <fstream>
using namespace std;

int main() {
    // Open file in both read and write mode
    fstream file("random_access.txt", ios::in | ios::out);

    if (!file) {
        cout << "File could not be opened!" << endl;
        return 1;
    }

    // Move the file pointer to the 5th byte (position 4)
    file.seekg(4);
    char ch;
    file.get(ch);  // Read the character at the 5th position
    cout << "Character at position 5: " << ch << endl;
```

```
    // Move the file pointer to the 10th byte (position 9)
    file.seekp(9);
    file.put('X');   // Write 'X' at the 10th position

    file.close();   // Close the file

    return 0;
}
```

Summary

- **File Handling in C++**:
  - **ifstream**: Used for reading from files.
  - **ofstream**: Used for writing to files.
  - **fstream**: Used for both reading and writing to files.
  - Operations such as reading, writing, and random access can be performed using the file stream classes.
- **Random Access in Files**:
  - The `seekg()` and `seekp()` functions allow you to move the file pointer to specific positions in the file.
  - `tellg()` and `tellp()` return the current positions of the file pointers for reading and writing, respectively.

C++ provides powerful file handling capabilities for both sequential and random access to files, making it a versatile language for managing file I/O.

Preprocessor Directives in C++

Preprocessor directives are instructions that are processed by the preprocessor before the actual compilation of the C++ program begins. These directives are not part of the C++ language itself but help control the compilation process, include files, define constants or macros, and conditionally compile code.

Common Preprocessor Directives in C++

1. #include

- **Purpose**: This directive is used to include header files or other source files in the program. The included files provide declarations of functions, classes, and other definitions that are necessary for the program to work.
- **Syntax**:

```
#include <iostream>  // Standard library inclusion
#include "myHeader.h"  // User-defined header file inclusion
```

- o **<iostream>**: Standard header file for input/output operations.
- o **"myHeader.h"**: User-defined header file, typically used to include custom declarations.

2. #define

- **Purpose**: The #define directive is used to define constants or macros that will be substituted in the code at the preprocessor stage. It does not require a data type for the constant.
- **Syntax**:

```
#define PI 3.14159  // Define a constant
#define SQUARE(x) ((x) * (x))  // Define a macro for squaring a number
```

- o **PI**: This defines the constant PI with the value 3.14159.
- o **SQUARE(x)**: This defines a macro SQUARE(x) that calculates the square of x when used in the code.

3. #ifdef and #ifndef

- **Purpose**: These directives are used to check if a macro is defined (#ifdef) or not defined (#ifndef). This is useful for conditional compilation, especially in large programs or libraries.
- **Syntax**:

```
#ifdef PI
    // Code to execute if PI is defined
#endif

#ifndef PI
    // Code to execute if PI is not defined
#endif
```

- o **#ifdef PI**: This checks if the macro PI has been defined. If true, the code inside the #ifdef block will be executed.
- o **#ifndef PI**: This checks if the macro PI has not been defined. If true, the code inside the #ifndef block will be executed.

4. #if, #else, #elif

- **Purpose**: These directives are used for conditional compilation based on the value of a constant or expression. It is commonly used for platform-specific code or versioning in large projects.
- **Syntax**:

```
#if defined(PI)
    // Code to execute if PI is defined
#else
    // Code to execute if PI is not defined
#endif
```

- o **#if**: Checks if a condition is true. If it is, the code inside the block is compiled.
- o **#else**: Provides an alternative block of code if the #if condition is false.
- o **#elif**: Stands for "else if" and is used to check multiple conditions in sequence.

5. #undef

- **Purpose**: The #undef directive is used to undefine a macro that was previously defined using #define. This allows you to cancel or modify a macro definition in the middle of a program.
- **Syntax**:

```
#define PI 3.14159
#undef PI  // Undefine the PI macro
```

- o **#undef PI**: This removes the definition of the macro PI, making it undefined.

Example of Using Preprocessor Directives

```
#include <iostream>
using namespace std;

#define PI 3.14159
#define SQUARE(x) ((x) * (x))

int main() {
    // Using defined constant and macro
    cout << "Value of PI: " << PI << endl;
    cout << "Square of 5: " << SQUARE(5) << endl;

    // Conditional compilation based on PI definition
    #ifdef PI
        cout << "PI is defined!" << endl;
    #endif

    #ifndef E
        cout << "E is not defined!" << endl;
    #endif

    // Undefining PI and checking its status
    #undef PI
    #ifdef PI
        cout << "PI is still defined!" << endl;
    #else
        cout << "PI is now undefined!" << endl;
```

```
    #endif

    return 0;
}
```

Summary

- **#include**: Used to include header files or other source files.
- **#define**: Defines constants or macros for reuse throughout the program.
- **#ifdef/#ifndef**: Used for conditional compilation, depending on whether a macro is defined or not.
- **#if, #else, #elif**: Used for conditional compilation based on expressions or values.
- **#undef**: Used to undefine a macro, making it no longer available.

These preprocessor directives are powerful tools for writing portable, maintainable, and efficient C++ programs.

Using Macros in C++

A macro in C++ is a preprocessor directive that defines code snippets that can be reused throughout the program. Macros are expanded by the preprocessor before compilation, replacing the macro with its definition. This allows you to use the macro in various places in your code, making the code more flexible and reducing redundancy.

Types of Macros

1. Macro for Constants

A macro can be used to define a constant value that can be used across the program.

- **Syntax**:

```
#define MAX_SIZE 100   // Define a constant
int arr[MAX_SIZE];   // Use MAX_SIZE as an array size
```

- **Explanation**:
  o **#define MAX_SIZE 100**: Defines a macro named MAX_SIZE with a value of 100.
  o **int arr[MAX_SIZE]**;: Declares an array with size 100 using the macro.

2. Macro for Functions

Macros can also define functions or expressions. These macros allow code to be reused without writing the same logic multiple times.

- **Syntax**:

```
#define SQUARE(x) ((x) * (x))   // Define a macro for squaring a
number
int result = SQUARE(5);   // Expands to ((5) * (5))
```

- **Explanation**:
  - **#define SQUARE(x) ((x) * (x))**: Defines a macro SQUARE(x) that computes the square of a number.
  - **SQUARE(5)**: This call will expand to ((5) * (5)) during preprocessing, and the result will be 25.

Important Considerations with Macros

While macros are powerful tools in C++, there are some important considerations when using them:

1. **Macros are not type-safe**:
   - Macros don't check the type of arguments, which can lead to unexpected behavior or errors. For example, passing non-numeric arguments to a macro designed for numbers may produce incorrect results.
2. **Parentheses are important**:
   - When defining macros that take arguments, always use parentheses around the arguments and the entire expression to ensure correct evaluation order.
   - For example, #define SQUARE(x) ((x) * (x)) ensures that the expression is evaluated correctly, even if x is an expression like a + b.

Example of Using Macros in C++

```
#include <iostream>
using namespace std;

#define MAX_SIZE 100   // Define a constant for array size
#define SQUARE(x) ((x) * (x))   // Define a macro to square a number

int main() {
    // Using the MAX_SIZE macro to declare an array
    int arr[MAX_SIZE];
    cout << "Array of size " << MAX_SIZE << " created!" << endl;

    // Using the SQUARE macro to square a number
    int number = 5;
    cout << "Square of " << number << " is " << SQUARE(number) << endl;
```

```
        return 0;
}
```

Summary

- **File Handling**:
  - o `ifstream`, `ofstream`, and `fstream` are the classes for handling file input/output.
  - o These classes allow you to perform operations like reading, writing, and random access in files.
- **Preprocessor Directives**:
  - o `#include`: Includes libraries or files in the program.
  - o `#define`: Defines constants or macros to reuse in code.
  - o `#ifdef`, `#ifndef`: Used for conditional compilation based on whether a macro is defined or not.
- **Macros**:
  - o Macros are used to define constants or functions that can be reused across the program.
  - o They enhance code readability, flexibility, and modularity but come with considerations like lack of type safety and the need for proper use of parentheses.

Preprocessor directives like macros play a crucial role in making C++ code more flexible, modular, and efficient. By using macros, you can define reusable code snippets and constants that improve the maintainability of the code.

25 MCQ ON THESE TOPICS

1. File Handling (fstream, ifstream, ofstream, and fstream Classes)

1. Which header file is required for file handling in C++?
   a) `<file>`
   b) `<fstream>`
   c) `<iostream>`
   d) `<iomanip>`
   Answer: b
2. Which class is used to create and write to files in C++?
   a) `ifstream`
   b) `ofstream`
   c) `fstream`
   d) `file`
   Answer: b

3. What does the `ifstream` class represent?
   a) Input file stream for reading files
   b) Output file stream for writing files
   c) File stream for both reading and writing
   d) Random file access
   Answer: a
4. To perform both read and write operations on a file, you would use:
   a) `ifstream`
   b) `ofstream`
   c) `fstream`
   d) `fileio`
   Answer: c
5. What is the correct syntax to open a file in `ofstream` mode?
   a) `ofstream file("filename.txt");`
   b) `ifstream file.open("filename.txt");`
   c) `ofstream file.open("filename.txt");`
   d) `fstream file("filename.txt", ios::out);`
   Answer: a

2. Reading and Writing Text Files

6. Which function is used to read data from a file?
   a) `getline()`
   b) `put()`
   c) `write()`
   d) `insert()`
   Answer: a
7. How do you check if a file has been successfully opened?
   a) Using `file.check()`
   b) Using `file.is_open()`
   c) Using `file.verify()`
   d) Using `file.status()`
   Answer: b
8. Which stream object is used to write data into a file?
   a) `cin`
   b) `ofstream`
   c) `cout`
   d) `ifstream`
   Answer: b
9. What happens if you try to open a non-existent file with `ifstream`?
   a) The program crashes.
   b) A new file is created.
   c) The stream is marked as failed.

d) An exception is thrown.
Answer: c

10. Which of the following correctly writes the string `"Hello"` to a file?
    a) `file << "Hello";`
    b) `file.write("Hello");`
    c) `write(file, "Hello");`
    d) `file << write("Hello");`
    Answer: a

3. Random Access in Files

11. Which function is used to move the file pointer to a specific location?
    a) `moveg()`
    b) `seekp()`
    c) `setp()`
    d) `pointer()`
    Answer: b

12. To get the current position of the file pointer, which function is used?
    a) `getp()`
    b) `tellg()`
    c) `locp()`
    d) `seekg()`
    Answer: b

13. What is the purpose of `seekg()`?
    a) Move the output pointer
    b) Move the input pointer
    c) Close the file
    d) Read a line from the file
    Answer: b

14. What does the `ios::app` mode do when opening a file?
    a) Opens the file for writing and appends data to the end.
    b) Opens the file for random access.
    c) Opens the file in binary mode.
    d) Opens the file for reading.
    Answer: a

15. What happens when you open a file with `ios::trunc` mode?
    a) The file is opened for reading.
    b) The existing content of the file is deleted.
    c) The file is opened in binary mode.
    d) The file pointer is moved to the end of the file.
    Answer: b

4. Preprocessor Directives (#include, #define, #ifdef, #ifndef, etc.)

16. What does the `#include` directive do?
    a) Links external libraries
    b) Includes the contents of another file
    c) Compiles the code
    d) Replaces a macro
    Answer: b

17. What is the purpose of the `#define` directive?
    a) Define a new data type
    b) Define symbolic constants and macros
    c) Include libraries
    d) Reserve memory
    Answer: b

18. Which preprocessor directive is used to include a file only once?
    a) `#once`
    b) `#only`
    c) `#pragma once`
    d) `#include`
    Answer: c

19. Which of the following is used to check if a macro is defined?
    a) `#if`
    b) `#ifndef`
    c) `#ifdef`
    d) `#endif`
    Answer: c

20. What does the `#ifndef` directive do?
    a) Checks if a file is included
    b) Checks if a macro is not defined
    c) Checks for syntax errors
    d) Ends a macro definition
    Answer: b

5. Using Macros

21. Which of the following defines a macro in C++?
    a) `define PI 3.14`
    b) `#define PI 3.14`
    c) `macro PI = 3.14`
    d) `#macro PI = 3.14`
    Answer: b

22. Which directive is used to undefine a macro?
    a) `#undef`
    b) `#undefine`

c) `#remove`

d) `#clear`

Answer: a

23. Which preprocessor directive allows conditional compilation?

    a) `#if`

    b) `#define`

    c) `#macro`

    d) `#compile`

    Answer: a

24. Which of the following is an invalid macro definition?

    a) `#define MAX 100`

    b) `#define SUM(a, b) ((a) + (b))`

    c) `#define PI 3.14`

    d) `define MAX 100`

    Answer: d

25. What is the primary purpose of macros?

    a) Allocate memory dynamically

    b) Replace code snippets during compilation

    c) Perform runtime calculations

    d) Optimize binary file size

    Answer: b

CHAPTER-9

USING CLASSES IN C++

C++, **classes** serve as a blueprint for creating objects. They enable the application of **Object-Oriented Programming (OOP)** principles. C++ supports essential OOP concepts, such as **Encapsulation**, **Abstraction**, **Inheritance**, and **Polymorphism**. These principles help developers design efficient, modular, and reusable code.

Let's explore these concepts in detail:

---

1. Principles of Object-Oriented Programming (OOP)

Object-Oriented Programming (OOP) is a programming paradigm that organizes software design around **objects** rather than functions and logic. An object is an instance of a class, which defines a collection of properties (data members) and methods (functions). The core principles of OOP in C++ are:

1.1 Encapsulation

- **Definition**: Encapsulation is the concept of bundling data (variables) and methods (functions) that operate on that data within a single unit, i.e., a class. It also restricts direct access to some of the object's components to ensure a controlled interaction with the data.
- **Explanation**: Encapsulation protects the integrity of the data by controlling how it is accessed or modified. This is done using **access specifiers** such as **private**, **protected**, and **public**. The private members of a class can only be accessed within the class, while public members are accessible from outside the class.
- **Example**:

```
class Person {
private:
    string name; // Private data member
    int age;
public:
    // Setter function to control the modification of private data
    void setName(string n) {
        name = n;
    }

    // Getter function to access the private data
    string getName() {
        return name;
    }
```

```
        // Setter and Getter for age
        void setAge(int a) {
            age = a;
        }
        int getAge() {
            return age;
        }
};

int main() {
    Person p;
    p.setName("John");
    p.setAge(30);
    cout << p.getName() << " is " << p.getAge() << " years old." <<
endl;
    return 0;
}
```

- **Outcome**: In this example, the `name` and `age` data members are private, meaning they can only be modified and accessed using public setter and getter methods, enforcing control over how the data is managed.

1.2 Abstraction

- **Definition**: Abstraction is the concept of hiding the **complex details** of an object and exposing only the **necessary parts**. This helps the programmer focus on high-level functionality without worrying about the internal workings.
- **Explanation**: Abstraction is achieved by using abstract classes or interfaces in C++. It helps reduce complexity by only showing essential features and hiding implementation details. It is often combined with encapsulation.
- **Example**:

```
class Shape {
public:
    virtual void draw() = 0;  // Pure virtual function (abstract
method)
};

class Circle : public Shape {
public:
    void draw() override {
        cout << "Drawing a Circle." << endl;
    }
};

class Square : public Shape {
public:
    void draw() override {
        cout << "Drawing a Square." << endl;
    }
```

```
};

int main() {
    Shape* shape1 = new Circle();
    Shape* shape2 = new Square();

    shape1->draw(); // Output: Drawing a Circle.
    shape2->draw(); // Output: Drawing a Square.

    delete shape1;
    delete shape2;
    return 0;
}
```

- **Outcome**: In this example, `Shape` is an abstract class with a pure virtual function `draw()`. The `Circle` and `Square` classes provide their own implementation of the `draw()` function, thereby abstracting the drawing process and allowing for different shapes without needing to know the specific implementation.

1.3 Inheritance

- **Definition**: Inheritance allows one class (child or subclass) to inherit the properties and behaviors (data members and member functions) of another class (parent or superclass). It promotes code reusability and establishes a hierarchical relationship between classes.
- **Explanation**: C++ supports single and multiple inheritance, where a subclass can inherit from one or more classes. The derived class can access public and protected members of the base class.
- **Example**:

```
class Animal {
public:
    void speak() {
        cout << "Animal is speaking!" << endl;
    }
};

class Dog : public Animal { // Dog class inherits from Animal
public:
    void bark() {
        cout << "Dog is barking!" << endl;
    }
};

int main() {
    Dog d;
    d.speak();  // Inherited method from Animal
    d.bark();   // Method of Dog class
    return 0;
}
```

- **Outcome**: In this example, the `Dog` class inherits from the `Animal` class and can use the `speak()` function. The `Dog` class also has its own method `bark()`. This demonstrates how inheritance allows a class to reuse functionality from its parent class.

- **Definition**: Polymorphism allows objects of different classes to be treated as objects of a common superclass. The most common use of polymorphism is when a base class pointer or reference is used to call methods of derived classes, allowing different behaviors depending on the type of the object being referenced.
- **Explanation**: Polymorphism is typically achieved through **function overriding** and **virtual functions**. It allows a derived class to provide a specific implementation of a method that is already defined in the base class.
- **Example**:

```cpp
class Base {
public:
    virtual void show() {  // Virtual function for polymorphism
        cout << "Base class show function" << endl;
    }
};

class Derived : public Base {
public:
    void show() override {  // Overriding the base class function
        cout << "Derived class show function" << endl;
    }
};

int main() {
    Base* basePtr;
    Derived derivedObj;
    basePtr = &derivedObj;

    basePtr->show();  // Output: Derived class show function
    return 0;
}
```

- **Outcome**: In this example, the `show()` function is **overridden** in the `Derived` class. The **virtual function** mechanism ensures that the method call to `show()` at runtime will call the appropriate function of the `Derived` class, even though the pointer is of type `Base`.

Class Constructors and Constructor Overloading

In C++, **constructors** are special member functions that are invoked when an object of a class is created. The primary purpose of a constructor is to **initialize** the object's data members. Constructors are automatically called at the time of object creation and do not require a function call.

Types of Constructors:

1. **Default Constructor**: A default constructor is a constructor that takes no parameters. If no constructor is defined in a class, the compiler provides a default constructor that initializes the data members to default values.
2. **Parameterized Constructor**: A parameterized constructor is a constructor that accepts one or more parameters. It allows the programmer to initialize the object with specific values at the time of its creation.

Syntax for Constructors:

```cpp
class ClassName {
private:
    int age;
public:
    // Default constructor
    ClassName() {
        age = 0;  // Initialize age to a default value
    }

    // Parameterized constructor
    ClassName(int a) {
        age = a;  // Initialize age with provided value
    }

    void displayAge() {
        cout << "Age: " << age << endl;
    }
};

int main() {
    ClassName obj1;         // Calls default constructor
    ClassName obj2(30);     // Calls parameterized constructor

    obj1.displayAge();  // Output: Age: 0
    obj2.displayAge();  // Output: Age: 30

    return 0;
}
```

- **Default Constructor**: The constructor `ClassName()` initializes the `age` to 0 when no arguments are passed during object creation.
- **Parameterized Constructor**: The constructor `ClassName(int a)` initializes the `age` to the provided value `a` when an argument is passed.
- **Constructor Overloading**: This feature allows a class to have more than one constructor with different parameters. In this case, we have two constructors: one without parameters (default) and one with a parameter (parameterized).

4. Function Overloading in Classes

Function Overloading in C++ is a feature that allows multiple functions to have the same name, but with different parameter lists. The function signature is different based on the number or type of parameters, and the appropriate function is called based on the arguments passed.

Example of Function Overloading:

```cpp
class Calculator {
public:
    // Function to add two integers
    int add(int a, int b) {
        return a + b;
    }

    // Overloaded function to add three integers
    int add(int a, int b, int c) {
        return a + b + c;
    }
};

int main() {
    Calculator calc;
    cout << "Sum of 2 numbers: " << calc.add(3, 4) << endl;      // Calls
add(int, int)
    cout << "Sum of 3 numbers: " << calc.add(3, 4, 5) << endl;    // Calls
add(int, int, int)
    return 0;
}
```

Explanation:

- **Function Overloading**: In this example, the `add()` function is overloaded with two versions:
  - One that accepts two integers (`add(int a, int b)`).
  - One that accepts three integers (`add(int a, int b, int c)`).

- **Function Resolution**: The correct version of the `add()` function is chosen based on the number of arguments passed when the function is called. If two arguments are provided, the first function is called; if three arguments are provided, the second function is invoked.

Key Points on Function Overloading:

- **Parameter Differentiation**: Function overloading is based on differences in the number of parameters, type of parameters, or both.
- **Return Type Doesn't Matter**: Overloading cannot be done just by changing the return type of the function. The function signature (parameter list) must be different for overloading to work.
- **Compile-time Resolution**: The C++ compiler determines which function to call based on the number and types of arguments during the compilation process.

Summary of Key Concepts:

1. **Class Constructors**:
   - **Default Constructor**: Initializes object with default values.
   - **Parameterized Constructor**: Allows initialization with specific values.
   - **Constructor Overloading**: Multiple constructors with different parameters can be defined.
2. **Function Overloading**:
   - Same function name can be used with different parameter lists (number or type).
   - Resolves the appropriate function to call based on the parameters passed.
   - Improves code readability and flexibility by allowing functions with similar behavior but different input.

Both constructor and function overloading enhance the flexibility and readability of code, allowing a more nat

Access Specifiers: Protected and Private

In C++, **access specifiers** determine the accessibility of the members (variables and functions) of a class. They define how and where the data members and methods of a class can be accessed. There are three types of access specifiers in C++:

1. Public:

- Members declared as `public` are accessible from anywhere in the program. They can be accessed both inside the class and outside the class.

2. Private:

- Members declared as `private` are accessible only within the class itself. They cannot be accessed from outside the class, including from derived classes.

3. Protected:

- Members declared as `protected` are accessible within the class and its derived (subclass) classes. However, they are not accessible outside the class hierarchy.

Example:
```cpp
class Person {
private:
    string name;  // Private member, accessible only within the class
protected:
    int age;  // Protected member, accessible within the class and derived
classes
public:
    void setName(string n) {
        name = n;
    }
    string getName() {
        return name;
    }
};
```
Explanation:

- **Private Members**: The `name` variable is private, meaning it cannot be accessed directly outside the `Person` class. The `setName` and `getName` methods provide public access to modify and retrieve the value of `name`.
- **Protected Members**: The `age` variable is protected, meaning it cannot be accessed directly outside the class, but it can be accessed by classes that derive from `Person`.
- **Public Members**: The `setName` and `getName` methods are public, which allows external code to modify or retrieve the `name` of a `Person` object.

6. Copy Constructors

A **copy constructor** in C++ is a special type of constructor that initializes a new object as a copy of an existing object. It is called when:

- A new object is created from an existing object of the same class.
- An object is passed by value to a function or returned by value from a function.

Syntax of Copy Constructor:
```cpp
class ClassName {
public:
```

```
    int value;

    // Default constructor
    ClassName(int val) {
        value = val;
    }

    // Copy constructor
    ClassName(const ClassName &obj) {
        value = obj.value;   // Copy the value from the existing object
    }
};

int main() {
    ClassName obj1(10);      // Creating object obj1
    ClassName obj2 = obj1;   // Creating object obj2 as a copy of obj1

    cout << "Value of obj2: " << obj2.value << endl;   // Output: 10

    return 0;
}
```

Explanation:

- **Default Constructor:** The `ClassName(int val)` constructor initializes an object with the value provided as an argument.
- **Copy Constructor:** The `ClassName(const ClassName &obj)` constructor creates a new object by copying the value of `obj.value` into the new object. This ensures that a new instance is created with the same value as the original object.
- **Usage in Main:** In the `main()` function, `obj2` is initialized as a copy of `obj1` using the copy constructor. The value of `obj2` will be the same as `obj1` (10 in this case).

When is the Copy Constructor Used?

1. **Object Initialization:** When an object is initialized with another object of the same type.

   ```
   ClassName obj2 = obj1; // Copy constructor is called
   ```

2. **Passing by Value:** When an object is passed by value to a function.

   ```
   void func(ClassName obj) { }
   func(obj1); // Copy constructor is called
   ```

3. **Returning by Value:** When an object is returned by value from a function.

   ```
   ClassName func() {
       ClassName obj(5);
       return obj; // Copy constructor or move constructor is called
   }
   ```

Deep vs. Shallow Copy:

- **Shallow Copy**: The default copy constructor performs a shallow copy. This means that if the object has pointers, the pointer values will be copied instead of the objects they point to. This can lead to issues such as multiple objects pointing to the same memory, causing data corruption or memory leaks.
- **Deep Copy**: In some cases, a **deep copy** is required. This involves explicitly writing a copy constructor that creates copies of dynamically allocated memory to avoid shared references. This ensures that each object has its own independent memory allocation.

Example of Deep Copy Constructor:

```
class MyClass {
private:
    int* data;

public:
    // Constructor
    MyClass(int val) {
        data = new int(val);  // Dynamically allocated memory
    }

    // Copy Constructor for Deep Copy
    MyClass(const MyClass &obj) {
        data = new int(*(obj.data));  // Allocates new memory and copies
value
    }

    ~MyClass() {
        delete data;  // Deallocates memory
    }
};
```

In this example, the copy constructor performs a deep copy by allocating new memory for `data` instead of just copying the pointer, ensuring that each object has its own unique memory location.

Summary:

1. **Access Specifiers**: Determine the visibility and accessibility of class members.
   - `private`: Accessible only within the class.
   - `protected`: Accessible within the class and derived classes.
   - `public`: Accessible from anywhere in the program.
2. **Copy Constructor**:
   - Used to create a new object as a copy of an existing object.
   - Ensures that an object is properly copied without affecting the original object, especially when dynamic memory is involved.

Overview of Template Classes in C++

Template classes in C++ allow for the creation of generic classes that can operate on different data types. Templates provide a mechanism for writing code that works with any data type, eliminating the need for duplication and improving code reusability.

What is a Template Class?

A **template class** is a blueprint for creating classes or functions with placeholders for data types. You can define a template with a **type parameter** (or **template parameter**) that will be replaced with a specific type when an object of the class is created.

Templates enable you to write generic and reusable code. With templates, you can define a class or function that can work with any data type without having to rewrite the same code for each type.

Syntax of Template Class

```
template <typename T>  // Define template with a type parameter T
class Box {
private:
    T value;  // The data type of 'value' is determined by the type passed
to the template
public:
    void setValue(T v) {  // The type of parameter 'v' is also determined
by the template
        value = v;
    }

    T getValue() {  // The return type of the function is determined by
the template
        return value;
    }
};
```

Explanation:

1. **template <typename T>**: This defines a template class with a placeholder for a data type T. The typename keyword is used to specify that T will be replaced by a specific type when the class is instantiated.
2. **T value;**: The type of the value member is T, which means it will be determined when the class is instantiated with a specific type.
3. **void setValue(T v)**: The setValue function accepts a parameter of type T and assigns it to the value member.
4. **T getValue()**: The getValue function returns a value of type T.

```
#include <iostream>
using namespace std;

template <typename T>  // Define template with a type parameter T
class Box {
private:
    T value;  // The data type of 'value' is determined by the type passed
to the template
public:
    void setValue(T v) {
        value = v;
    }

    T getValue() {
        return value;
    }
};

int main() {
    Box<int> intBox;        // Create a Box for int type
    Box<double> doubleBox; // Create a Box for double type

    intBox.setValue(10);   // Set an integer value to intBox
    doubleBox.setValue(3.14); // Set a double value to doubleBox

    cout << "Int box: " << intBox.getValue() << endl;  // Output: 10
    cout << "Double box: " << doubleBox.getValue() << endl;  // Output:
3.14

    return 0;
}
```

Explanation of the Example:

1. **Creating Template Objects**:
   - `Box<int> intBox;`: This creates an object `intBox` of type `Box` where `T` is replaced with `int`.
   - `Box<double> doubleBox;`: This creates another object `doubleBox` of type `Box` where `T` is replaced with `double`.
2. **Setting Values**:
   - `intBox.setValue(10);`: This calls the `setValue` function for `intBox`, passing an integer value (`10`).
   - `doubleBox.setValue(3.14);`: This calls the `setValue` function for `doubleBox`, passing a double value (`3.14`).
3. **Getting Values**:
   - `cout << "Int box: " << intBox.getValue() << endl;`: This prints the value stored in the `intBox` object, which is `10`.
   - `cout << "Double box: " << doubleBox.getValue() << endl;`: This prints the value stored in the `doubleBox` object, which is `3.14`.

- **Code Reusability**: Templates allow you to write a single class definition that can handle different types, making the code reusable and avoiding duplication.
- **Type Safety**: Templates ensure that the data type used in the class is consistent throughout the program. This means that if you use a `Box<int>`, it will always expect and return `int` values.
- **Flexibility**: Templates provide the flexibility to define classes and functions that can work with any data type, including user-defined types (e.g., classes, structs).

Template Specialization

C++ allows you to specialize templates for specific data types. This is called **template specialization** and allows you to provide a different implementation for certain data types while keeping the general template intact.

Example of Template Specialization:

```cpp
#include <iostream>
using namespace std;

template <typename T>
class Box {
private:
    T value;
public:
    void setValue(T v) {
        value = v;
    }
    T getValue() {
        return value;
    }
};

// Specialization for char type
template <>
class Box<char> {
private:
    char value;
public:
    void setValue(char v) {
        value = v;
    }
    char getValue() {
        return value;
    }
    void display() {
        cout << "Specialized Box for char: " << value << endl;
    }
};

int main() {
    Box<int> intBox;
```

```
    Box<char> charBox;

    intBox.setValue(100);
    charBox.setValue('A');

    cout << "Int Box: " << intBox.getValue() << endl;
    charBox.display(); // Special function for char type

    return 0;
}
```
Explanation:

- The `Box<char>` class is a **specialized template** where the template has been specialized to handle `char` data type differently.
- The `display` function is specific to the `Box<char>` class and demonstrates how you can modify the behavior of a template class for specific types.

---

25 MCQ ON THESE TOPICS

1. Principles of Object-Oriented Programming

1. What is the key principle of Object-Oriented Programming (OOP)?
   a) Procedural code structure
   b) Data abstraction and encapsulation
   c) Inline functions and macros
   d) Global variables
   Answer: b
2. Which of the following is NOT an OOP concept?
   a) Inheritance
   b) Polymorphism
   c) Encapsulation
   d) Compilation
   Answer: d
3. What does encapsulation in OOP refer to?
   a) Hiding data implementation and exposing only necessary details
   b) Using functions for complex logic
   c) Combining header files
   d) Using classes for object creation
   Answer: a
4. Which of the following best defines polymorphism?
   a) Combining two or more data types
   b) Defining multiple functions with the same name but different signatures
   c) Using a single name for multiple classes
   d) Reusing code from a base class
   Answer: b

5. What is inheritance in OOP?
   a) Defining multiple constructors
   b) Accessing private variables
   c) Acquiring properties and behaviors of a base class in a derived class
   d) Creating inline functions
   Answer: c

2. Defining and Using Classes

6. What is a class in C++?
   a) A group of functions
   b) A user-defined data type that holds data members and member functions
   c) A built-in type in C++
   d) A structure with additional features
   Answer: b

7. How do you declare an object of a class?
   a) `className objectName;`
   b) `class className objectName;`
   c) `objectName = new className;`
   d) `objectName(className);`
   Answer: a

8. Which of the following is NOT a valid member of a class?
   a) Public functions
   b) Private variables
   c) Protected variables
   d) Standalone main() function
   Answer: d

9. What keyword is used to define a class in C++?
   a) `object`
   b) `struct`
   c) `class`
   d) `type`
   Answer: c

10. How do you access a public member of a class?
    a) `objectName->memberName;`
    b) `className.memberName;`
    c) `objectName.memberName;`
    d) `className->memberName;`
    Answer: c

3. Class Constructors and Constructor Overloading

11. What is a constructor in C++?
    a) A function to destroy objects
    b) A function to initialize objects
    c) A function to manipulate data
    d) A destructor function
    Answer: b
12. What is the main feature of a default constructor?
    a) It takes one argument.
    b) It has no arguments.
    c) It returns a value.
    d) It is a static function.
    Answer: b
13. Which of the following is a characteristic of constructor overloading?
    a) Multiple constructors with the same number of arguments
    b) Multiple constructors with different numbers or types of arguments
    c) Constructors with return types
    d) Constructors with inline functions
    Answer: b
14. What happens if no constructor is defined in a class?
    a) The program throws an error.
    b) The compiler automatically generates a default constructor.
    c) The program cannot compile.
    d) The object cannot be created.
    Answer: b
15. Which of the following correctly defines a parameterized constructor?

```
class MyClass {
    public:
        MyClass(int x) { /*...*/ }
};
```

    a) `MyClass() {}`
    b) `MyClass(int x) {}`
    c) `MyClass() : int x {}`
    d) `MyClass(x : int) {}`
    Answer: b

4. Function Overloading in Classes

16. What is function overloading?
    a) Using multiple functions with the same name but different arguments
    b) Redefining a function in the derived class
    c) Overloading operators for a class
    d) Defining multiple classes with the same function
    Answer: a
17. Which of the following can differ in overloaded functions?
    a) Function name
    b) Return type
    c) Number and types of arguments
    d) Function call operator
    Answer: c
18. Can functions with the same name and the same arguments be overloaded if their return types are different?
    a) Yes
    b) No
    Answer: b

5. Access Specifiers: Protected and Private

19. What does the `private` access specifier mean?
    a) Accessible by all classes
    b) Accessible only by member functions of the same class
    c) Accessible by derived classes
    d) Accessible by global functions
    Answer: b
20. What is the purpose of the `protected` access specifier?
    a) Accessible only by the base class
    b) Accessible by derived classes and member functions of the base class
    c) Accessible by all classes
    d) Hidden from the derived class
    Answer: b

6. Copy Constructors

21. What is the purpose of a copy constructor?
    a) Initialize one object from another object of the same class
    b) Destroy an object
    c) Assign default values

d) Overload functions
Answer: a

22. How is a copy constructor defined?
    a) With a return type of `void`
    b) As a constructor that takes an object of the same class as an argument
    c) As a constructor with no arguments
    d) As a static function
    Answer: b

23. If no copy constructor is provided, what does the compiler do?
    a) Generates an error
    b) Creates a default copy constructor
    c) Refuses to create objects
    d) Throws a runtime exception
    Answer: b

7. Overview of Template Classes

24. What is a template class in C++?
    a) A class defined with placeholder types
    b) A class used only for inheritance
    c) A precompiled class
    d) A built-in class
    Answer: a

25. Which keyword is used to define a template class?
    a) `template`
    b) `generic`
    c) `placeholder`
    d) `define`
    Answer: a

CHAPTER-10

OVERVIEW OF FUNCTION OVERLOADING AND OPERATOR OVERLOADING IN C++

In C++, **function overloading** and **operator overloading** are features that allow multiple functions or operators to have the same name but with different parameters or behavior. These features provide the flexibility to work with different types of data, enhancing code readability and maintainability. Let's explore these concepts in detail.

---

1. Need for Overloading Functions and Operators

Function Overloading:

Function overloading enables the creation of multiple functions with the same name but different parameter lists. This is particularly useful when you want to perform similar operations on different types or numbers of arguments, reducing the need to create distinct function names for each case. It simplifies code and makes it more readable.

Operator Overloading:

Operator overloading allows the modification of operators (like +, -, *, etc.) to work with user-defined classes. By overloading operators, we can use the standard operators for custom types, making code easier to understand and use. This is similar to how operators work with built-in types, but now applied to user-defined types.

---

2. Overloading by Number and Type of Arguments

Function overloading works by changing the **number** and/or **type** of arguments in the function definition. The compiler differentiates between the overloaded functions based on the number or type of parameters passed during the function call.

Function Overloading Example:

```
#include <iostream>
using namespace std;

class Calculator {
public:
    // Function to add two integers
    int add(int a, int b) {
        return a + b;
    }
```

```
    // Function to add three integers
    int add(int a, int b, int c) {
        return a + b + c;
    }

    // Function to add two floating-point numbers
    double add(double a, double b) {
        return a + b;
    }
};

int main() {
    Calculator calc;
    cout << "Sum of 2 integers: " << calc.add(3, 4) << endl;
    cout << "Sum of 3 integers: " << calc.add(3, 4, 5) << endl;
    cout << "Sum of 2 doubles: " << calc.add(2.5, 3.5) << endl;

    return 0;
}
```

Explanation:

- The add function is overloaded to handle different parameter types and numbers:
    - **Two integers**: add(int, int)
    - **Three integers**: add(int, int, int)
    - **Two floating-point numbers (doubles)**: add(double, double)
- The compiler selects the appropriate function based on the number and type of arguments passed during the function call.

For example:

- calc.add(3, 4) will call add(int, int) and return the sum of the integers.
- calc.add(3, 4, 5) will call add(int, int, int) and return the sum of the three integers.
- calc.add(2.5, 3.5) will call add(double, double) and return the sum of the two floating-point numbers.

This mechanism of function overloading makes it easier to create more general and flexible functions that can handle multiple data types without needing separate function names.

Operator as Function Call in C++

In C++, operators are implemented as functions under the hood, meaning that when you overload an operator, you are essentially defining a special function that handles that specific operation. This allows you to use operators in a way that is more intuitive and flexible, especially for user-defined classes. Operator overloading enables the use of custom types in expressions just as you would with built-in types.Let's dive into the details of **operator overloading as a function call**.

Operator Overloading Concept

When you overload an operator in C++, you're telling the compiler how to perform the operation on instances of a class. Behind the scenes, the overloaded operator is treated as a function. The operator itself becomes a function call, with the operands acting as the arguments. This allows the operator to be customized for user-defined types, just like how built-in operators work for primitive types.

For example, when you use the + operator with two integers, the compiler internally calls a function that adds the two values. In a similar way, when you overload the + operator for a custom class, you're defining a function that handles the addition of two objects of that class.

Example of Operator Overloading:

Let's consider an example where we define a `Complex` class and overload the + operator to add two complex numbers.

```cpp
#include <iostream>
using namespace std;

class Complex {
private:
    float real;
    float imag;

public:
    // Default constructor
    Complex() : real(0), imag(0) {}

    // Parameterized constructor
    Complex(float r, float i) : real(r), imag(i) {}

    // Overloading the '+' operator
    Complex operator + (const Complex& obj) {
        Complex temp;
        temp.real = real + obj.real;  // Adding real parts
        temp.imag = imag + obj.imag;  // Adding imaginary parts
        return temp;
    }

    // Function to display the complex number
    void display() {
        cout << "Real: " << real << " Imag: " << imag << endl;
    }
```

```
};

int main() {
    Complex num1(3.5, 4.5), num2(1.5, 2.5);
    Complex result = num1 + num2;  // Calls overloaded '+' operator

    result.display();  // Output: Real: 5 Imag: 7
    return 0;
}
```

Explanation of the Code:

1. **Class Definition:**
   - The `Complex` class represents complex numbers with two private members: `real` (for the real part) and `imag` (for the imaginary part).
   - There are two constructors: a default constructor that initializes the complex number to `0 + 0i`, and a parameterized constructor that allows setting custom real and imaginary values.
2. **Operator Overloading:**
   - The `operator +` function is the key part of operator overloading in this example. It allows us to use the + operator to add two `Complex` objects.
   - The function takes another `Complex` object as a parameter (`const Complex& obj`) and performs the addition by adding the real and imaginary parts separately:
     - `temp.real = real + obj.real;`
     - `temp.imag = imag + obj.imag;`
   - The result is returned as a new `Complex` object.
3. **Function Call Mechanism:**
   - When `num1 + num2` is executed in the `main()` function, it calls the overloaded `operator +` function. The operands `num1` and `num2` are passed as arguments to this function.
   - Inside the function, the real and imaginary parts of the two complex numbers are added, and the result is returned as a new `Complex` object, which is stored in the `result` variable.
4. **Displaying the Result:**
   - The `display()` function is called on `result` to print the sum of the complex numbers.
   - The output is `Real: 5 Imag: 7`, which is the sum of the real and imaginary parts of `num1` and `num2`.

Why Operator Overloading is Like a Function Call:

In this example, the + operator is overloaded as a function:

- The syntax `num1 + num2` translates internally to a call to the overloaded function `operator +` with `num1` and `num2` as the arguments.

- The function returns a new `Complex` object with the result of the addition, which is assigned to the `result` variable.

This behavior is similar to how you would call a normal function, where the operator itself acts as a function and is executed accordingly. This provides the flexibility to extend the functionality of operators to custom types and makes the code more intuitive and readable.

perator Overloading Example (with Custom Types):

Consider another example where we overload the $<<$ operator for outputting a custom class:

```cpp
#include <iostream>
using namespace std;

class Point {
private:
    int x, y;
public:
    Point(int x, int y) : x(x), y(y) {}

    // Overloading the '<<' operator for custom output
    friend ostream& operator <<(ostream& out, const Point& p) {
        out << "(" << p.x << ", " << p.y << ")";
        return out;
    }
};

int main() {
    Point p1(5, 6);
    cout << "Point: " << p1 << endl;   // Calls overloaded '<<' operator
    return 0;
}
```

Output:

```
Point: (5, 6)
```

In this example, the $<<$ operator is overloaded to display the `Point` class objects in a human-readable format. When you write `cout << p1`, the overloaded `operator <<` function is called.

Conclusion:

Operator overloading treats operators as function calls, giving you the ability to define custom behavior for operators in user-defined classes. By overloading operators, you can make your custom types behave like built-in types, improving code readability and maintainability. The concept of operator overloading as function calls allows a seamless integration of user-defined types with standard C++ operations.

Overloading Operators (Assignment and Unary Operators)

In C++, operator overloading allows you to redefine the behavior of operators for user-defined classes. Two important operators that are commonly overloaded are the **assignment operator (=)** and **unary operators** (e.g., increment ++, decrement --). Let's explore both types of operator overloading in detail.

A. Assignment Operator Overloading:

The assignment operator (=) is used to copy one object's state into another. In C++, the default assignment operator performs a **shallow copy**. This means that if the object contains pointers or dynamically allocated memory, both objects (the original and the assigned) will point to the same memory location, which could lead to unintended side effects, such as double deletion of memory during object destruction.

To prevent this issue, **assignment operator overloading** is used to perform a **deep copy**. This ensures that the dynamically allocated memory is properly copied, and each object gets its own separate memory.

Example of Assignment Operator Overloading:

Here's a detailed example of overloading the assignment operator for a class that contains a pointer to dynamically allocated memory:

```
#include <iostream>
using namespace std;

class MyClass {
private:
    int* ptr;

public:
    // Constructor to allocate memory
```

```cpp
    MyClass(int val) {
        ptr = new int;
        *ptr = val;
    }

    // Overloading assignment operator
    MyClass& operator = (const MyClass& obj) {
        if (this == &obj) return *this;  // Handle self-assignment

        delete ptr;  // Deallocate old memory
        ptr = new int;  // Allocate new memory
        *ptr = *(obj.ptr);  // Perform deep copy
        return *this;  // Return *this to allow chained assignments
    }

    // Function to display the value stored in ptr
    void display() {
        cout << "Value: " << *ptr << endl;
    }

    // Destructor to free dynamically allocated memory
    ~MyClass() {
        delete ptr;
    }
};

int main() {
    MyClass obj1(10);  // Create object with value 10
    MyClass obj2(20);  // Create object with value 20

    obj2 = obj1;  // Overloaded assignment operator

    obj1.display();  // Output: Value: 10
    obj2.display();  // Output: Value: 10

    return 0;
}
```

Explanation of the Code:

1. **Constructor:**
   o   The constructor `MyClass(int val)` dynamically allocates memory to store an integer and initializes it with the given value `val`.
2. **Overloaded Assignment Operator (`operator=`):**
   o   The assignment operator is overloaded to handle deep copying. First, the `if (this == &obj)` check is used to handle **self-assignment** (i.e., when an object is assigned to itself).
   o   If the objects are not the same, we delete the existing memory (`delete ptr`) to avoid memory leaks and then allocate new memory (`ptr = new int`).
   o   The value of the other object is copied (`*ptr = *(obj.ptr)`), ensuring that the objects do not share the same memory.

- The operator returns `*this`, which allows for **chained assignments** (e.g., `a = b = c`).
3. **Destructor:**
   - The destructor `~MyClass()` ensures that the dynamically allocated memory is properly deallocated when an object is destroyed, preventing memory leaks.
4. **Output:**
   - After the assignment `obj2 = obj1;`, the values of `obj1` and `obj2` are both `10`, demonstrating that a deep copy was performed.

B. Unary Operator Overloading:

Unary operators are operators that operate on a single operand. Examples include increment (++), decrement (--), logical NOT (!), and unary minus (-).

In C++, both **prefix** and **postfix** versions of unary operators (e.g., ++ and --) can be overloaded. The difference between the prefix and postfix versions is that the postfix version requires a temporary object to store the original value before performing the operation.

Example of Unary Operator Overloading (Prefix and Postfix):

Here's how you can overload the increment operator (++) for both **prefix** and **postfix** versions:

```
#include <iostream>
using namespace std;

class Counter {
private:
    int count;

public:
    // Constructor to initialize count
    Counter() : count(0) {}

    // Overloading prefix ++
    Counter& operator++() {
        ++count;  // Increment count
        return *this;  // Return the incremented object
    }

    // Overloading postfix ++
```

```cpp
    Counter operator++(int) {
        Counter temp = *this;   // Create a copy of the current object
        ++count;   // Increment count
        return temp;   // Return the original object (before increment)
    }

    // Function to display the current count
    void display() {
        cout << "Count: " << count << endl;
    }
};

int main() {
    Counter c1;
    ++c1;   // Calls prefix ++
    c1.display();   // Output: Count: 1

    c1++;   // Calls postfix ++
    c1.display();   // Output: Count: 2

    return 0;
}
```

Explanation of the Code:

1. **Prefix Increment (++c1):**
   - The prefix ++ operator is overloaded in the function `Counter& operator++()`. This version increments the `count` first and then returns a reference to the updated object (`*this`).
   - This allows the operation to modify the current object and return the updated object directly.
2. **Postfix Increment (c1++):**
   - The postfix ++ operator is overloaded in the function `Counter operator++(int)`. The `int` parameter is a dummy parameter used to distinguish the postfix version from the prefix version.
   - In the postfix version, a temporary `Counter` object (`temp`) is created to store the current state of the object before incrementing.
   - After incrementing the `count`, the original object (the one before the increment) is returned.
3. **Output:**
   - The program demonstrates both versions of the increment operator. After the prefix increment `++c1`, the count is 1. After the postfix increment `c1++`, the count becomes 2.

Key Points:

- **Assignment Operator Overloading:**

- It is essential for handling deep copying, especially when the class contains dynamic memory. The overloaded assignment operator ensures that the class behaves correctly when objects are assigned to each other.
- Always handle **self-assignment** (e.g., `if (this == &obj)`), and return `*this` for chained assignments.
- **Unary Operator Overloading:**
  - The **prefix** version of the operator directly modifies and returns the object.
  - The **postfix** version creates a temporary copy, increments the value, and returns the original object (before the increment).

Both assignment and unary operator overloading help provide more natural and intuitive behavior when working with user-defined types, allowing them to behave like built-in types when using standard operators.

25 MCQ ON THESE TOPICS

1. Need for Overloading Functions and Operators

1. Why is function overloading useful in C++?
   a) It allows using different names for functions.
   b) It allows defining multiple functions with the same name but different arguments.
   c) It enables functions to have different return types.
   d) It prevents function duplication.
   Answer: b
2. What is the primary purpose of operator overloading in C++?
   a) To increase the number of operators available in the language
   b) To allow custom behavior for operators in user-defined classes
   c) To modify the behavior of built-in operators only
   d) To provide a default implementation for operators
   Answer: b
3. Which of the following is NOT a reason to use function overloading?
   a) To provide multiple implementations of a function
   b) To improve code readability
   c) To define multiple functions with the same name but different types of arguments
   d) To create a more complex function
   Answer: d
4. In operator overloading, what is the key reason for defining custom behavior for operators?
   a) To increase the number of operators in C++
   b) To make operators work with user-defined classes
   c) To change the syntax of operators
   d) To define new types of operators
   Answer: b

2. Overloading by Number and Type of Arguments

5. Function overloading is based on the difference in:
   a) Return type only
   b) Function body
   c) Number and type of arguments
   d) Access specifiers
   Answer: c

6. What happens if two overloaded functions have the same number and type of arguments?
   a) The compiler throws an error
   b) The compiler selects the one that appears first
   c) The compiler chooses the one with a different return type
   d) The compiler cannot distinguish between them
   Answer: d

7. Which of the following is an example of function overloading by type of arguments?
   a) `void add(int, int)` and `void add(float, float)`
   b) `void add(int)` and `void add(int)`
   c) `void add(int, int)` and `void add(int)`
   d) `void add(int)` and `void add(void)`
   Answer: a

8. Can a function be overloaded with different numbers of arguments?
   a) Yes, as long as the arguments are of the same type
   b) Yes, as long as the function names are different
   c) Yes, by varying the number of arguments
   d) No, it is not allowed in C++
   Answer: c

9. Which of the following function signatures are valid examples of overloading by number of arguments?
   a) `void func(int)` and `void func(int, float)`
   b) `void func(int, float)` and `void func(int)`
   c) `void func(int)` and `void func(int, float)`
   d) All of the above
   Answer: d

10. Can two overloaded functions have the same parameter types but different return types?
    a) Yes
    b) No
    Answer: b

3. Operator as Function Call

11. What does it mean to treat an operator as a function call in C++?
    a) Defining the operator's behavior using a function syntax

b) Using operators directly within function arguments

c) Replacing the operator with a function name

d) Treating the operator as a built-in function

Answer: a

12. How does operator overloading affect the way operators are used in C++?

a) It modifies the syntax of operators.

b) It allows user-defined classes to use operators as function calls.

c) It introduces new operators in C++.

d) It changes the priority of operators.

Answer: b

13. When an operator is overloaded as a function, which syntax is used?

a) `operator <`

b) `operator overload`

c) `function operator()`

d) `operator function`

Answer: a

14. What is a key advantage of using operator overloading with function calls?

a) It reduces the complexity of the operator

b) It simplifies operator use in user-defined classes

c) It adds new operators to the language

d) It enhances operator precedence

Answer: b

15. Which of the following statements about operator overloading is true?

a) Operator overloading cannot be done for assignment operators

b) Overloaded operators must behave similarly to built-in operators

c) Operators cannot be overloaded with function calls

d) Overloading operators always requires a return type

Answer: b

4. Overloading Operators (Assignment and Unary Operators)

16. Which of the following operators can be overloaded in C++?

a) Assignment operator

b) Unary operators (e.g., ++, --)

c) Both

d) Neither

Answer: c

17. Which keyword is used to overload an assignment operator in C++?

a) `operator=`

b) `operator+`

c) `function=`

d) `overload=`

Answer: a

18. What does the assignment operator (=) do when overloaded?
    a) It assigns values between two objects of the same class
    b) It compares values between two objects
    c) It creates a new object
    d) It performs a mathematical operation on two objects
    Answer: a

19. Which of the following is a valid example of overloading the unary ++ operator?
    a) `void operator++()`
    b) `int operator++(int)`
    c) `void operator++(int)`
    d) `int operator++()`
    Answer: b

20. When overloading the ++ operator, which version should be used for a postfix increment?
    a) `operator++()`
    b) `operator++(int)`
    c) `operator++(void)`
    d) `operator++(float)`
    Answer: b

21. Which of the following statements is true regarding the overloading of the assignment operator?
    a) The overloaded assignment operator must return a reference to the object
    b) The overloaded assignment operator can return a value
    c) The overloaded assignment operator cannot be used with user-defined classes
    d) The assignment operator cannot be overloaded in C++
    Answer: a

22. Which of the following statements about overloading unary operators is true?
    a) Unary operators can be overloaded with a single parameter
    b) Unary operators must be overloaded with two parameters
    c) Unary operators cannot be overloaded in C++
    d) Unary operators require a return type when overloaded
    Answer: a

23. Which of the following operators cannot be overloaded in C++?
    a) Assignment operator
    b) Increment operator
    c) Subscript operator (`[]`)
    d) Scope resolution operator (`::`)
    Answer: d

24. What is the main purpose of overloading the = operator in C++?
    a) To assign new values to an object
    b) To compare two objects for equality
    c) To define how two objects are initialized
    d) To copy an object from one instance to another
    Answer: d

25. Which of the following is NOT a valid reason to overload an operator?
    a) To make operators compatible with user-defined types

b) To improve code readability and ease of use
c) To introduce new operators in C++
d) To provide customized behavior for operators in user-defined classes
Answer: c

CHAPTER-11

INHERITANCE IN C++: DEFINITION, TYPES, CONCEPTS, AND EXPLANATION

Inheritance is one of the fundamental principles of **Object-Oriented Programming (OOP)**. It allows a new class (called a derived class) to inherit the properties and behaviors (data members and member functions) from an existing class (called a base class). This leads to code reusability, and also enables the creation of more complex hierarchies of classes.

Inheritance represents an **"is-a"** relationship between the base class and the derived class. For example, a **Dog** is a type of **Animal**, so **Dog** can inherit from **Animal**.

Inheritance can be of different types based on how a derived class is related to base classes.

Types of Inheritance in C++

1. **Single Inheritance:**
   - In **single inheritance**, a class derives from only one base class. This is the simplest form of inheritance.
   - **Concept**: A derived class inherits properties and methods from a single base class.
   - **Example**: A **Dog** class inherits from an **Animal** class.

   Example:

```cpp
#include <iostream>
using namespace std;

class Animal {
public:
    void speak() {
        cout << "Animal speaks!" << endl;
    }
};

class Dog : public Animal {
public:
    void bark() {
        cout << "Dog barks!" << endl;
    }
};

int main() {
    Dog d;
    d.speak();  // Inherited from Animal
    d.bark();   // Dog-specific method

    return 0;
}
```

Explanation:

- o Dog inherits from `Animal`. So, a `Dog` object can call the `speak()` method, which is inherited from the `Animal` class. Additionally, it has its own method `bark()`.

---

2. **Multi-Level Inheritance:**
   - o **Multi-level inheritance** is when a class inherits from a derived class, forming a chain of inheritance. In this case, a class is derived from another derived class.
   - o **Concept**: A class inherits from a class that has already inherited from another class.
   - o **Example**: A **Grandchild** class inherits from a **Child** class, and the **Child** class inherits from a **Parent** class.

Example:

```cpp
#include <iostream>
using namespace std;

class Animal {
public:
    void speak() {
        cout << "Animal speaks!" << endl;
    }
};

class Mammal : public Animal {
public:
    void walk() {
        cout << "Mammal walks!" << endl;
    }
};

class Dog : public Mammal {
public:
    void bark() {
        cout << "Dog barks!" << endl;
    }
};

int main() {
    Dog d;
    d.speak();  // Inherited from Animal
    d.walk();   // Inherited from Mammal
    d.bark();   // Dog-specific method

    return 0;
}
```

Explanation:

- o **Multi-level inheritance:** The `Dog` class inherits from `Mammal`, and `Mammal` inherits from `Animal`.
- o The `Dog` object can access methods from both `Mammal` and `Animal` (i.e., `speak()` from `Animal`, `walk()` from `Mammal`, and `bark()` from `Dog`).

---

3. **Multiple Inheritance:**
   - o **Multiple inheritance** occurs when a class derives from more than one base class. This allows the derived class to inherit properties and methods from multiple base classes.
   - o **Concept:** A class can access methods and properties from more than one parent class.
   - o **Example:** A **FlyingCar** class might inherit from both the **Car** class and the **Airplane** class.

Example:

```cpp
#include <iostream>
using namespace std;

class Car {
public:
    void drive() {
        cout << "Car is driving!" << endl;
    }
};

class Airplane {
public:
    void fly() {
        cout << "Airplane is flying!" << endl;
    }
};

class FlyingCar : public Car, public Airplane {
public:
    void transform() {
        cout << "Flying car transforms!" << endl;
    }
};

int main() {
    FlyingCar fc;
    fc.drive();    // Inherited from Car
    fc.fly();      // Inherited from Airplane
    fc.transform(); // FlyingCar-specific method

    return 0;
}
```

Explanation:

     o **Multiple inheritance**: The `FlyingCar` class inherits from both `Car` and `Airplane`. This allows the `FlyingCar` object to use the `drive()` method from `Car`, `fly()` method from `Airplane`, and its own `transform()` method.

Concept of Inheritance in C++

- **Access Specifiers**: The inheritance relationship in C++ is influenced by the access specifiers (`public`, `protected`, and `private`) used in the derived class.
  - **Public Inheritance**: The members of the base class are accessible as they are in the derived class.
  - **Private Inheritance**: The members of the base class are not accessible outside the derived class (only internally).
  - **Protected Inheritance**: The members of the base class are accessible within the derived class and its subclasses, but not outside.

Benefits of Inheritance:

1. **Code Reusability**: It allows you to reuse the code of an existing class without rewriting it.
2. **Extensibility**: You can create new classes based on existing classes, extending their functionality.
3. **Hierarchical Classification**: It helps in organizing classes in a hierarchical structure.

Polymorphism in C++: Definition, Types, Concepts, and Explanation

Polymorphism is one of the key principles of Object-Oriented Programming (OOP) in C++, which allows objects of different types to be treated as objects of a common base type. It enables a single function, method, or operator to operate in multiple ways depending on the context, enhancing flexibility and code reuse.

Polymorphism is classified into two main types in C++:

1. **Compile-time Polymorphism** (also called **Static Polymorphism**): Achieved through function overloading and operator overloading.
2. **Runtime Polymorphism** (also called **Dynamic Polymorphism**): Achieved through virtual functions and function overriding.

Here, we'll focus on **runtime polymorphism**, which is enabled using **virtual functions**.

1. Virtual Functions (Runtime Polymorphism)

Virtual functions enable the feature of **runtime polymorphism**. A virtual function is a function in the base class that can be overridden by derived classes. When a function is declared as **virtual**, the compiler ensures that the correct function (i.e., the function from the derived class) is called at runtime, based on the actual object type, not the pointer type.

Concept:

- When a function is called through a **base class pointer** or reference, and the function is overridden in the derived class, the function from the **derived class** is executed, even though the base class type is used. This is called **dynamic dispatch** or **late binding**.
- This behavior allows for more flexible and extensible designs, where new classes can override base class functions to provide specific implementations without changing the client code.

Example of Virtual Function (Runtime Polymorphism)

```cpp
#include <iostream>
using namespace std;

class Animal {
public:
    // Virtual function
    virtual void speak() {
        cout << "Animal speaks!" << endl;
    }
};

class Dog : public Animal {
public:
    // Overriding the base class function
    void speak() override {
        cout << "Dog barks!" << endl;
    }
};

int main() {
    // Create an object of Dog
    Animal* animal = new Dog();

    // Call speak() using a base class pointer
    animal->speak();  // Calls Dog's version of speak

    delete animal;  // Clean up
    return 0;
}
```

Explanation of the Example:

- **Base Class (`Animal`)**:
  - The class `Animal` has a member function `speak()`. It is declared as `virtual`, meaning it can be overridden in any derived class.
- **Derived Class (`Dog`)**:
  - The class `Dog` inherits from `Animal` and overrides the `speak()` function to provide its own behavior.
- **Main Function**:
  - A pointer of type `Animal*` is created, but it points to an object of type `Dog`.
  - When `animal->speak()` is called, the `speak()` method from the `Dog` class is executed, even though the pointer is of type `Animal*`. This is **runtime polymorphism** in action.
  - If we had used a `Dog*` pointer instead of an `Animal*` pointer, the result would have been the same because the object is still of type `Dog`. However, using the base class pointer here demonstrates polymorphism.
- **Key Points**:
  - The `virtual` keyword in the base class ensures that the function call is resolved at runtime based on the actual object type (`Dog` in this case), not the pointer type (`Animal*`).
  - The `override` keyword in the derived class (`Dog`) ensures that the function is correctly overriding the base class function and helps with compile-time checks.

Why Virtual Functions are Important?

- **Flexibility and Extensibility**: Virtual functions allow you to define a base class interface and then provide different implementations in the derived classes. This makes it easier to extend your program with new classes without changing existing code.
- **Late Binding**: The decision of which function to call is deferred until runtime, based on the actual object type, which makes it possible for derived classes to change or extend the behavior of base class methods.
- **Code Reusability**: Base class pointers or references can be used to refer to objects of different derived types, making code more reusable and modular.

Example with Multiple Derived Classes:

```
#include <iostream>
using namespace std;

class Animal {
public:
    virtual void speak() {
        cout << "Animal speaks!" << endl;
    }
```

```cpp
};

class Dog : public Animal {
public:
    void speak() override {
        cout << "Dog barks!" << endl;
    }
};

class Cat : public Animal {
public:
    void speak() override {
        cout << "Cat meows!" << endl;
    }
};

int main() {
    Animal* animal1 = new Dog();
    Animal* animal2 = new Cat();

    animal1->speak();  // Calls Dog's version of speak
    animal2->speak();  // Calls Cat's version of speak

    delete animal1;
    delete animal2;
    return 0;
}
```

Explanation:

- The same base class pointer (Animal*) is used to refer to objects of type Dog and Cat.
- When speak() is called on animal1, the version from Dog is called, and when speak() is called on animal2, the version from Cat is called.
- This demonstrates polymorphism in action with multiple derived classes.

Key Takeaways:

1. **Virtual Function**: The virtual keyword in C++ enables runtime polymorphism by allowing a method to be overridden in derived classes and enabling dynamic dispatch.
2. **Dynamic Dispatch**: The correct method is determined at runtime based on the actual object type, not the type of the pointer/reference.
3. **Flexibility**: Virtual functions make it possible to extend programs without changing existing code, making them a powerful tool for writing flexible and modular applications.
4. **Override**: The override keyword is used to mark methods in derived classes that are overriding base class methods, providing compile-time checks for correctness.

Summary of Polymorphism Types in C++

- **Compile-Time Polymorphism (Static Polymorphism)**: Achieved through function overloading and operator overloading. The function to call is determined at compile time.
- **Runtime Polymorphism (Dynamic Polymorphism)**: Achieved through virtual functions. The function to call is determined at runtime, based on the actual object type, not the pointer/reference type.

---

2. **Pure Virtual Functions**:
   - A **pure virtual function** is a virtual function that does not have a definition in the base class and forces derived classes to provide an implementation.
   - **Concept**: It makes the base class an **abstract class**, and the derived class must implement this function.

Example:

```cpp
#include <iostream>
using namespace std;

class Shape {
public:
    virtual void draw() = 0;   // Pure virtual function
};

class Circle : public Shape {
public:
    void draw() override {
        cout << "Drawing a circle!" << endl;
    }
};

int main() {
    Shape* shape = new Circle();
    shape->draw();   // Calls Circle's draw method

    delete shape;
    return 0;
}
```

Explanation:

- The draw() method is a pure virtual function in the Shape class, so Shape is abstract and cannot be instantiated. The derived class Circle must provide an implementation of draw().

Exception Handling in C++: Definition, Concepts, and Explanation

Exception handling in C++ provides a structured way to deal with unexpected or error conditions that may arise during program execution. Instead of allowing a program to terminate abruptly when an error occurs, exception handling allows the program to continue executing or to handle the error in a controlled manner.

In C++, exceptions are managed using three main components: **try**, **throw**, and **catch**. These components allow you to detect, throw, and handle exceptions.

---

1. Throwing Exceptions:

To throw an exception in C++, you use the **throw** keyword. The **throw** keyword is used to signal that an error or exception has occurred. You can throw various types of data as exceptions, such as integers, strings, or custom objects.

Syntax:
```
throw expression;
```

Here, `expression` is the object or value that represents the exception being thrown. The type of the expression can be anything, depending on the exception you want to throw (e.g., an integer, string, or custom exception type).

Example 1: Throwing an integer exception
```
#include <iostream>
using namespace std;

int main() {
    try {
        throw 404;  // Throws an integer exception with value 404
    } catch (int errorCode) {
        cout << "Caught exception: " << errorCode << endl;  // Catch and
print the integer exception
    }

    return 0;
}
```

Explanation:

- The `throw 404;` statement throws an integer exception with the value `404`.
- The `catch (int errorCode)` block catches this exception and prints the value of the error code.

Example 2: Throwing a string exception
```
#include <iostream>
using namespace std;
```

```cpp
int main() {
    try {
        throw "Error occurred";  // Throws a string exception
    } catch (const char* msg) {
        cout << "Caught exception: " << msg << endl;  // Catch and print
the string exception
    }

    return 0;
}
```

Explanation:

- The `throw "Error occurred";` statement throws a string exception.
- The `catch (const char* msg)` block catches the string exception and prints the message.

2. Catching Exceptions:

Once an exception is thrown, you need to catch it and handle it. This is done using the **catch** block. The **catch** block specifies the type of exception it handles and the variable used to store the exception object.

Syntax:
```cpp
try {
    // Code that may throw an exception
} catch (ExceptionType1 e1) {
    // Handle exception of type ExceptionType1
} catch (ExceptionType2 e2) {
    // Handle exception of type ExceptionType2
}
```

Here, the `catch` block can handle multiple types of exceptions, and it follows the `try` block.

Example: Catching multiple types of exceptions
```cpp
#include <iostream>
using namespace std;

int main() {
    try {
        int choice;
        cout << "Enter 1 for integer exception or 2 for string exception:
";
        cin >> choice;

        if (choice == 1) {
            throw 404;  // Integer exception
        } else if (choice == 2) {
            throw "Error occurred";  // String exception
```

```
        }
    } catch (int errorCode) {
        cout << "Caught integer exception: " << errorCode << endl;
    } catch (const char* msg) {
        cout << "Caught string exception: " << msg << endl;
    }

    return 0;
}
```

Explanation:

- The `try` block contains code that may throw different types of exceptions based on user input.
- The `catch (int errorCode)` block catches an integer exception and prints the error code.
- The `catch (const char* msg)` block catches a string exception and prints the message.

3. Handling Multiple Exceptions:

In C++, you can have multiple `catch` blocks to handle different types of exceptions. Each `catch` block catches a specific type of exception. You can also have a generic `catch` block that handles all exceptions of any type.

Example: Handling multiple types of exceptions with a generic catch block
```
#include <iostream>
using namespace std;

int main() {
    try {
        throw 404;   // Integer exception
    } catch (int e) {
        cout << "Caught integer exception: " << e << endl;
    } catch (...) {
        cout << "Caught an unknown exception!" << endl;   // Catch all
exceptions
    }

    return 0;
}
```

Explanation:

- The `catch (...)` block is a generic catch block that catches any type of exception not caught by the previous `catch` blocks.
- It is a good practice to use the generic `catch` block when you want to catch exceptions that do not match specific types.

4. Rethrowing Exceptions:

Once an exception is caught, you might want to pass it along to another part of the program for further handling. This is done by **rethrowing** the exception using the **throw** keyword inside a `catch` block.

Syntax:
```
catch (ExceptionType e) {
    // Handle exception
    throw;  // Rethrow the same exception
}
```
Example: Rethrowing exceptions
```cpp
#include <iostream>
using namespace std;

void function1() {
    try {
        throw "An error occurred";  // Throw exception
    } catch (const char* msg) {
        cout << "Caught exception in function1: " << msg << endl;
        throw;  // Rethrow the exception
    }
}

int main() {
    try {
        function1();  // Call function1 which throws and rethrows the
exception
    } catch (const char* msg) {
        cout << "Caught exception in main: " << msg << endl;    }

    return 0;}
```

Explanation:

- The exception "An error occurred" is thrown in `function1` and caught there.
- The `throw;` statement inside `catch` rethrows the same exception.
- The `catch` block in the `main` function catches the rethrown exception and prints the message.

Conclusion

- **Throwing Exceptions**: The `throw` keyword is used to signal that an error has occurred. You can throw various types of data (e.g., integers, strings, custom objects).
- **Catching Exceptions**: The `catch` block is used to handle exceptions. It matches the type of the exception thrown and executes the corresponding block of code.
- **Rethrowing Exceptions**: You can rethrow an exception using the `throw` keyword inside a `catch` block to pass the exception to higher levels of the program for further handling.

- **Handling Multiple Exceptions**: You can have multiple `catch` blocks to handle different types of exceptions, or use a generic `catch` block to catch all exceptions.

By using exception handling, you can ensure that your programs are more robust and can handle unexpected conditions gracefully without crashing.

C. Basics of Exception Handling (catch and throw)

Exception handling is a mechanism to handle runtime errors in C++ by using the `try`, `throw`, and `catch` blocks.

1. **`throw`**: Used to **throw** an exception.
2. **`try`**: Code that might throw an exception is placed inside a `try` block.
3. **`catch`**: Catches exceptions thrown by the `try` block.

Example:
```
#include <iostream>
using namespace std;

void divide(int a, int b) {
    if (b == 0) {
        throw "Division by zero error!";
    }
    cout << "Result: " << a / b << endl;
}

int main() {
    try {
        divide(10, 0);   // Will throw an exception
    } catch (const char* msg) {
        cout << "Exception caught: " << msg << endl;
    }

    return 0;
}
```
Explanation:

- In the `divide()` function, if `b` is 0, an exception is thrown using the `throw` keyword.
- The exception is caught in the `catch` block, and a message is printed to the user.

D. Handling Multiple Exceptions and Restricting Exceptions

C++ allows multiple `catch` blocks to handle different types of exceptions.

1. **Multiple Exceptions**: You can use multiple `catch` blocks to handle different exceptions.

2. **Restricting Exceptions**: You can restrict the type of exceptions caught by specifying the exception type in the `catch` block.

Example:
```cpp
#include <iostream>
using namespace std;

void testFunction(int num) {
    if (num < 0) {
        throw "Negative number exception!";
    } else if (num == 0) {
        throw 0;  // Integer exception
    } else {
        cout << "Number is positive!" << endl;
    }
}

int main() {
    try {
        testFunction(-1);  // Will throw a string exception
    } catch (const char* msg) {
        cout << "Caught: " << msg << endl;
    }

    try {
        testFunction(0);  // Will throw an integer exception
    } catch (int x) {
        cout << "Caught integer exception: " << x << endl;
    }

    return 0;
}
```
Explanation:

- The `testFunction()` can throw either a string or an integer exception.
- The `catch` blocks are designed to handle both types of exceptions: one for a string (`const char*`) and one for an integer (`int`).

E. Rethrowing Exceptions

Sometimes, after catching an exception, you might want to rethrow it for further processing by another part of the program. This is done using the `throw;` statement without specifying the exception type.

Example:
```cpp
#include <iostream>
using namespace std;

void function1() {
    try {
```

```
        throw 42;   // Throw an integer exception
    } catch (int e) {
        cout << "Caught exception in function1: " << e << endl;
        throw;   // Rethrow the exception
    }
}

int main() {
    try {
        function1();   // Function1 throws and rethrows an exception
    } catch (int e) {
        cout << "Caught exception in main: " << e << endl;
    }

    return 0;
}
```

Explanation:

- In the `function1()`, an integer exception is thrown and caught. After handling, the exception is rethrown using `throw;`.
- The `main()` function catches the rethrown exception and prints it.

---

25 MCQ ON THESE TOPICS

1. Introduction to Inheritance (Multi-Level and Multiple Inheritance)

1. Which of the following is a feature of inheritance in C++?
   a) Allows a new class to acquire properties of an existing class
   b) Prevents access to base class members
   c) Increases the complexity of the code
   d) None of the above
   Answer: a

2. What type of inheritance is shown when a class inherits from another class, which itself is derived from a base class?
   a) Single inheritance
   b) Multiple inheritance
   c) Multi-level inheritance
   d) Hierarchical inheritance
   Answer: c

3. Which of the following is true about multiple inheritance?
   a) A class can inherit from multiple classes
   b) A class can inherit from only one base class
   c) Multiple inheritance is not supported in C++
   d) A class cannot inherit from more than two classes
   Answer: a

4. What is a major disadvantage of multiple inheritance in C++?
   a) It causes ambiguity if a base class has a function that is inherited from more than one class
   b) It leads to larger memory usage
   c) It makes the code unreadable
   d) It limits code reuse
   Answer: a
5. In multi-level inheritance, how many base classes can a derived class have?
   a) One
   b) Two
   c) Three
   d) Multiple
   Answer: a
6. Which inheritance model does C++ support?
   a) Single inheritance only
   b) Multiple inheritance only
   c) Multi-level inheritance only
   d) Single, multi-level, and multiple inheritance
   Answer: d

2. Polymorphism: Virtual Functions and Pure Virtual Functions

7. What is polymorphism in C++?
   a) The ability of a class to inherit properties from multiple classes
   b) The ability to have different behaviors in different contexts
   c) The ability to use multiple functions with the same name
   d) The ability to assign multiple objects to a class
   Answer: b
8. What does a virtual function in C++ allow?
   a) Multiple functions with the same name in different classes
   b) Overriding a base class function in a derived class
   c) Defining functions with different return types
   d) Both a and b
   Answer: b
9. What is the purpose of the `virtual` keyword in C++?
   a) To prevent a function from being overridden in a derived class
   b) To allow a function in a base class to be overridden in a derived class
   c) To make a function accessible to other classes
   d) To declare a pure virtual function
   Answer: b
10. Which of the following is true about pure virtual functions?
    a) They have a default implementation
    b) They cannot be overridden
    c) They must be overridden in derived classes

d) They are optional to implement in derived classes
Answer: c

11. A class with at least one pure virtual function is considered:
    a) A concrete class
    b) A virtual class
    c) An abstract class
    d) A derived class
    Answer: c

12. What happens if a derived class does not override a pure virtual function?
    a) The code will compile without errors
    b) The program will throw an exception at runtime
    c) The derived class becomes abstract
    d) The base class function is automatically called
    Answer: c

3. Basics of Exception Handling (catch and throw)

13. In C++, which of the following keywords is used to handle exceptions?
    a) `throw`
    b) `catch`
    c) `try`
    d) All of the above
    Answer: d

14. What is the correct syntax to throw an exception in C++?
    a) `throw` followed by the exception object
    b) `throw` followed by a variable
    c) `throw` followed by a type
    d) `throw` followed by a function name
    Answer: a

15. What does the `catch` block in C++ do?
    a) It throws an exception
    b) It handles the exception thrown by the `throw` statement
    c) It prevents exceptions from being thrown
    d) It specifies the type of exceptions to be thrown
    Answer: b

16. Which of the following statements about exception handling in C++ is correct?
    a) Exception handling in C++ can be done using `throw`, `catch`, and `try` blocks
    b) Only one `catch` block is allowed per `try` block
    c) `catch` must be called before `throw`
    d) Exception handling is not allowed in C++
    Answer: a

17. Which statement is true regarding exception objects in C++?
    a) An exception object can be of any type
    b) An exception object must always be a pointer

c) An exception object can only be an integer
d) Exception objects are always automatically destroyed
Answer: a

4. Handling Multiple Exceptions and Restricting Exceptions

18. How can multiple exceptions be handled in C++?
    a) Using a single `catch` block for all exceptions
    b) Using multiple `catch` blocks after a `try` block
    c) Using a loop inside the `catch` block
    d) C++ does not support handling multiple exceptions
    Answer: b
19. What happens when multiple exceptions are thrown, but no matching `catch` block is found?
    a) The program continues execution
    b) The program crashes
    c) The program terminates gracefully
    d) An error message is displayed
    Answer: b
20. What is the best practice when handling multiple exceptions?
    a) Always catch every exception in a single block
    b) Catch only specific exceptions and rethrow others
    c) Use a `try` block without any `catch` block
    d) Handle exceptions in the main function only
    Answer: b
21. Which of the following restricts an exception in C++?
    a) Catching an exception before it is thrown
    b) Specifying the type of exception to catch
    c) Using `try` block without `catch`
    d) Throwing a `null` exception
    Answer: b
22. Can an exception be restricted to a specific block in C++?
    a) Yes, by using specific types in `catch`
    b) No, exceptions cannot be restricted
    c) Yes, by using global exception handling
    d) No, exceptions are handled globally
    Answer: a

5. Rethrowing Exceptions

23. What does rethrowing an exception mean in C++?
    a) Throwing an exception again after catching it
    b) Handling an exception multiple times
    c) Ignoring an exception
    d) Catching an exception in multiple places
    Answer: a

24. Which of the following is the correct syntax for rethrowing an exception in C++?
    a) `throw()`
    b) `catch()`
    c) `throw;`
    d) `catch;`
    Answer: c

25. What is the primary purpose of rethrowing an exception?
    a) To propagate the exception further up the call stack
    b) To ignore the exception
    c) To log the exception
    d) To handle the exception immediately
    Answer: a

www.ingramcontent.com/pod-product-compliance
Lightning Source LLC
LaVergne TN
LVHW081756050326

832903LV00027B/1964